# Grundwortschatz Deutsch
# Essential German

# Grundwortschatz Deutsch
# Essential German

compiled by Heinz Oehler

HARRAP LONDON

in association with

Ernst Klett Verlag Stuttgart

*First published in Great Britain 1968*
*by* HARRAP LIMITED
19–23 Ludgate Hill, London EC4M 7PD
*Reprinted* 1977; 1979; 1980; 1983


ISBN 0 245-59402-7

---

*Composed in Univers and Old Style types and printed and bound in Great Britain by William Clowes (Beccles) Limited Beccles and London*

## Contents

## Preface

This essential vocabulary in German is the result of more than 50 years' statistical linguistic survey in Germany, the United States, England and France.

From research into the frequency of word usage we know the following facts: more than 80% of the vocabulary of all normal texts is included in the basic 1000 words of a language; a further 8 to 10% in the second 1000, approximately 4% in the third 1000, a further 2% in the fourth and likewise another 2% in the fifth. Thus, the first 4000 words comprise on an average 95% of the vocabulary of all normal texts and dialogues, the second 4000 about 2 to 3%, and all other words not more than 1 to 2%.

This basic vocabulary offers more than 2000 basic words and 3000 idioms in German with their English equivalents. For those who want to learn the vocabulary of everyday German or to consolidate their word power, it will be indispensable. Once this knowledge has been acquired, one can understand German and make oneself adequately understood in German.

The material for this basic vocabulary is the generally spoken, written and printed language of our day. The work contains the results of German, Anglo-Saxon and French research into word frequency: for German we have drawn on the conclusions of Kaeding, Bakonyi, Schultze, Michéa, Wängler and lastly on those of Meier and Pfeffer; for English on the conclusions of West, Thorndike, Palmer, Ogden, Haase and Weis (see Bibliography).

A comparison of German basic vocabulary with that of English shows a surprising degree of conformity; most basic words and idioms are to be found in both languages. In the present basic vocabulary only very few words had to be omitted on the grounds that they had no equivalent in the other language. Names of people, towns, animals, plants, drinks, illnesses were not included if there were no counterparts in the basic vocabulary of English or if they cannot be recognized as belonging to the basic vocabulary of German, for example the words *doll, Sekt, Forelle, Veilchen, Knecht, Masern.*

The practical value of a word depends not only on its frequency, but just as much on the extent of its meaning and its expressive value. Frequency of use could not, therefore, be the only criterion of choice. As well as the linguistic statistician the language teacher has also had his say; from his teaching experience he could and had to supplement and correct what catalogue, punched card, tape recorder and more recently the computer had recorded.

## Abbreviations

| | | | |
|---|---|---|---|
| acc | *accusative* | m | *masculine* |
| adj | *adjective* | mod AV | *modal auxiliary verb* |
| adv | *adverb* | n | *neuter* |
| adv prn | *adverbial pronoun* | o's | *one's* |
| am | *American* | o.s. | *oneself* |
| art | *article* | pass | *passive* |
| AV | *auxiliary verb* | past part | *past participle* |
| card | *cardinal number* | perf | *perfect* |
| cf | *compare* | pers | *person* |
| cond | *conditional* | pers prn | *personal pronoun* |
| conj | *conjunction* | pl | *plural* |
| dat | *dative* | pluperf | *pluperfect* |
| dem prn | *demonstrative pronoun* | poss prn | *possessive pronoun* |
| det prn | *determinative pronoun* | pres | *present tense* |
| etw | etwas (*something*) | pret | *preterite* |
| f | *feminine* | prn | *pronoun* |
| fut | *future* | prp | *preposition* |
| gen | *genitive* | refl prn | *reflexive pronoun* |
| ger | *gerund* | rel prn | *relative pronoun* |
| imp | *imperative* | s | *substantive* |
| ind prn | *indefinite pronoun* | sg | *singular* |
| jdm | jemandem (*to someone*) | s.o. | *someone* |
| jdn | jemanden (*someone*) | s.o.'s | *someone's* |
| | | s.th. | *something* |
| | | v | *verb* |

## Explanations and signs

1. The stress in words of two or more syllables is shown by an accent (ˈ); the syllable following the accent is stressed (ˈDeutschland).
2. If the the genitive singular of a noun has a special ending, this follows the noun (der Deutsche *n*: des Deutsche*n*; das Land *es*; des Land*es*).
3. After a diagonal stroke (/) the nominative plural ending of a noun is given (der Deutsche n/*n*: die Deutsche*n*).
   A hyphen after the diagonal stroke indicates that the noun has no nominative plural ending (der Lehrer s/-: der Lehrer, des Lehrers/die Lehrer).
   Nouns without a diagonal stroke or hyphen after them exist only in the singular (der Mut (e)s; die Liebe; das Blut (e)s).
4. Where there is vowel modification (Umlaut) in the plural, the modified vowel appears followed by the plural ending (das Land es/*ä-er*: die L*ä*nd*er*).
5. Where vowels are modified in the comparative and superlative forms, the three forms appear individually (h*o*ch / h*ö*her / am h*ö*chsten).
6. The vowel modification in strong (irregular) verbs follows the verb in question (fallen *ie-a*/*ä*); thus we have the root vowel for the Preterite (*ie* for f*ie*l) and for the Perfect Participle (*a* for gef*a*llen) and the modified vowel for the 2nd and 3rd person of the Present after the diagonal stroke (/*ä* for f*ä*llst, f*ä*llt).
7. If a particle is separable from the verb, it is shown by a vertical stroke (|) (*an*|fangen: ich fange *an*).
8. Antonyms of nouns, adjectives and verbs are shown by (→): (Leid → Freude, tief → hoch, fallen → steigen).

## Strukturwörter/Structural words

Structural words are the most frequent words in a language; approximately half an average text is made up of them. They qualify and replace the noun (article, pronoun, numeral), indicate word relationship (preposition) and circumstances (adverb), join parts of speech and sentences (conjunction) and determine the inner structure of the whole sentence. (For practical reasons adverbs have been included in the basic vocabulary itself.)

| | |
|---|---|
| **aber** conj | but, however |
| **als** conj | when; than; as |
| **am = an dem** | |
| **an** prp + dat, acc | at; on; upon; by; against; to; in |
| **auf** prp + dat, acc | (up)on; in; at; of; by; to; for |
| **aus** prp + dat | out (of); from; of; by; through; (up) on; in; off |
| **außer** prp + dat | out of, outside; beyond, beside(s), apart from, save, except for |
| **außer daß/wenn** conj | except/save/but that; if not; unless |
| **außerhalb** prp + gen | out of; outside, beyond |
| **bei** prp + dat | near, by; of; at; in; with; on; next to |
| **beim = bei dem** | |
| **bevor** conj | before |
| **bezüglich** prp + gen / **mit Bezug auf, in bezug auf** | concerning, as to, regarding, with regard to |
| **bis (nach / ab / zu)** prp ; conj | till, until; to, up to |
| **da** conj | as, because |

| | |
|---|---|
| **da'mit** conj | (in order) that, in order to |
| **das** art | the |
| **das = dies(es)** dem prn | that, this; it |
| **das = welches** rel prn | which; that |
| **das, was** det prn | that which |
| **daß** conj | that |
| **dein,e** poss prn | your |
| **deine(r,s)** | yours |
| **denn** conj | for |
| **der** art | the |
| **der = dieser** dem prn | this, that; he, it |
| **der = welcher** rel prn | who, which; that |
| **dich** pers prn acc (of **du**) | you |
| **die** art | the |
| **die = diese** dem prn | this, that; these, those; she, her; they, them |
| **die = welche** rel prn | who, which, that; whom, which, that |
| **die(jenige), welche** det prn | she who/whom |
| **diejenigen, welche** det prn | they/those who/whom |
| **dies,e** dem prn | this, that; these, those |
| **dir** pers prn dat (of **du**) | (to) you |
| **du** pers prn | you |
| **durch** prp + acc | through, across; by; by means of |
| **ehe** conj | before |
| **ein,e** art | a(n) |
| **eine(r,s)** card | one |
| **entgegen** prp + dat | against; towards |
| **entlang** (an) prp + dat | along |
| **entsprechend** prp + gen | corresponding to |
| **entweder . . . oder** conj | either . . . or |
| **er** pers prn | he, it |
| **es** pers prn | it |
| **es sei denn, daß** | unless |

| | |
|---|---|
| **euch** pers prn dat, acc (of **ihr**) | you, (to you) |
| **euer, eure** poss prn | your |
| **eure(r,s)** | yours |
| **falls** conj | if; in case |
| **für** prp + acc | for; in exchange for; instead of; on behalf of; in favour of; for the sake of |
| **gegen** prp + acc | against; toward(s); about, by; compared with |
| **gemäß** prp + dat | according to |
| **haben** AV (perf, pluperf) | to have . . . |
| **hinter** prp + dat, acc | behind; after |
| **ich** pers prn | I |
| **ihm** pers prn dat (of **er**) | (to) him/it |
| **ihn** pers prn acc (of **er**) | him, it |
| **ihr** pers prn pl | you |
| **ihr** pers prn sg dat (of **sie**) | (to) her |
| **ihr,e** poss prn sg, pl | her; their |
| **ihre(r,s)** | hers; theirs |
| **Ihr,e** poss prn (cf. **Sie**) | your |
| **im** = **in dem** | |
| **in** prp + dat, acc | in, at, on, within, into, during |
| **indem** conj | as, while, whilst; by |
| **infolge** prp + gen | as a result of, in consequence of, owing to |
| **innerhalb** prp + gen | within |
| **ins** = **in das** | |
| **längs** prp + gen | along |
| **mein,e** poss prn | my |
| **meine(r,s)** | mine |
| **mich** pers prn acc (of **ich**) | me |
| **mir** pers prn dat (of **ich**) | (to) me |

| | |
|---|---|
| **mit** prp + dat | with; by (means of) |
| **nach** prp + dat | to(wards), for; after, past, at the end of, in; according to |
| **nachdem** conj | after, when |
| **neben** prp + dat, acc | by the side of, beside, by, close by, near to, next to; besides |
| **nicht nur . . . , sondern auch** conj | not only . . . but also |
| **ob** conj | if, whether |
| **obwohl, obgleich** conj | (al)though |
| **oder** conj | or |
| **ohne** prp + acc | without |
| **ohne daß** conj | without (+ *ger*) |
| **quer durch / über** prp + acc | across |
| **sei es . . ., sei es** conj | whether . . . or |
| **sein** AV (perf, pluperf) | to have . . . |
| **sein,e** poss prn | his, its |
| **seine(r,s)** | his, its |
| **seit** prp + dat; conj | since |
| **seitens** prp + gen | on the part of, by |
| **sich** refl prn | oneself; himself, herself, itself; themselves; him, her, it, them; each other, one another |
| **sie** pers prn sg, pl | she, her; they, them |
| **Sie** pers prn sg, pl | you |
| **sobald (wie/als)** conj | as soon as |
| **so daß** conj | so that, so as to |
| **soll** mod AV pres | shall, am/is to |
| **sollte** mod AV pret; cond | should, was to; ought to |
| **sondern** conj | but |
| **sonst** conj | otherwise, else |
| **so'weit** | as much as, as far as |

| | |
|---|---|
| **sowohl . . . als auch** conj | both . . . and, as well as; not only . . . but (also) |
| **statt, anstatt** prp + gen | instead of |
| **statt daß** conj | instead of |
| **trotz** prp + gen, dat | in spite of, despite, notwithstanding |
| **trotzdem** conj | although, notwithstanding that |
| **über** prp + dat, acc | over; above; across; by way of (via); beyond, past; at, of, on |
| **um** prp + acc | at; near, towards; by; for |
| **um . . . herum** | (round) about |
| **um so (besser)** | so much the (better) |
| **um zu** | in order to |
| **und** conj | and |
| **uns** pers prn dat, acc (of **wir**) | (to) us |
| **unser,e** poss prn | our |
| **unsere(r,s)** | ours |
| **unter** prp + dat, acc | under; below, beneath; in; between; among, amid(st) |
| **vom** = **von dem** | |
| **von** prp + dat | of; from; by |
| **vor** prp + dat, acc | before, in front of; before; of, with; because of; from |
| **während** prp + gen; conj | during; while, whilst; as |
| **was** rel prn | what, that, which |
| **weder . . . noch** conj | neither . . . nor |
| **wegen** prp + gen | because of, for; by reason of, owing to, concerning |

| | |
|---|---|
| **weil** conj | because, as; since |
| **welche(r,s)** rel prn | who, which; that |
| **welche(s)** ind prn | some, any |
| **wenn** conj | when; if, in case |
| **wenn nicht** | if not; unless |
| **wer** rel prn | who, he who |
| **werden** AV (fut, pass, cond) | (shall, will); to be going to; to be |
| **wider** prp + acc | against, contrary to |
| **wie** conj | as |
| **wir** pers prn | we |
| **wird** (cf **werden**) | |
| **worauf** prn adv | on which, after which, whereupon |
| **woraus** prn adv | from which, out of which, whence |
| **worin** adv prn | in which, wherein |
| **worüber** adv prn | over/upon which, about which |
| **würde** (cf. **werden**) | |
| **zu** prp + dat; conj | to, at, in, on; for; towards, up to; along with; beside |
| **zum = zu dem** | |
| **zur = zu der** | |
| **zwischen** prp + dat, acc | between |

## Grundzahlen/Cardinal numbers

| | | | |
|---|---|---|---|
| **eins** | one | **neun** | nine |
| **zwei** | two | **zehn** | ten |
| **drei** | three | **elf** | eleven |
| **vier** | four | **zwölf** | twelve |
| **fünf** | five | **'dreizehn** | thirteen |
| **sechs** | six | **'vierzehn** | fourteen |
| **'sieben** | seven | **'fünfzehn** | fifteen |
| **acht** | eight | **'sechzehn** | sixteen |

| | | | |
|---|---|---|---|
| 'siebzehn | seventeen | 'fünfzig | fifty |
| 'achtzehn | eighteen | 'sechzig | sixty |
| 'neunzehn | nineteen | 'siebzig | seventy |
| 'zwanzig | twenty | 'achtzig | eighty |
| 'dreißig | thirty | 'neunzig | ninety |
| 'vierzig | forty | 'hundert | a hundred |

## Ordnungszahlen/Ordinal numbers

| | |
|---|---|
| der/die/das 'erste | the first |
| der/die/das 'zweite | the second |
| der/die/das 'dritte | the third |
| 'vierte | fourth |
| 'fünfte | fifth |
| 'sechste | sixth |
| 'siebte, siebente | seventh |
| 'achte | eighth |
| 'neunte | ninth |
| 'zehnte | tenth |

| | |
|---|---|
| 'erstens | first(ly) |
| 'zweitens | second(ly) |
| 'drittens | third(ly) |
| 'viertens | fourth(ly) |
| 'fünftens | fifth(ly) |
| 'sechstens | sixth(ly) |
| 'siebtens, siebentens | seventh(ly) |
| 'achtens | eighth(ly) |
| 'neuntens | ninth(ly) |
| 'zehntens | tenth(ly) |

## Grundwortschatz/Basic vocabulary

### A

| | |
|---|---|
| **ab** | off, down; away; from |
| *ab und zu* | *now and again* |
| **der 'Abend** s/e | evening |
| *am Abend* | *in the evening* |
| *eines Abends* | *one evening* |
| *gegen Abend* | *towards evening* |
| *heute abend* | *this evening, tonight* |
| *gestern abend* | *yesterday evening* |
| *morgen abend* | *tomorrow evening* |
| **das 'Abendessen** s/- | dinner, supper |
| *zu Abend essen* | *to have dinner* |
| **'abends** | in the evening |
| *von morgens bis abends* | *from morning to night* |
| **'ab\|fahren** u-a/ä → ankommen | to leave, to start |
| **die 'Abfahrt** /en | departure |
| **'ab\|hängen (von)** i-a | to depend (on) |
| *abhängig* | *dependent* |
| *es hängt von ihm ab* | *it's up to him* |
| **'ab\|holen** | to come for, to meet |
| *ich hole dich ab* | *I'll come to meet you/ call for you* |
| **'ab\|laden** u-a/ä → beladen | to unload |
| **'ab\|machen** → offenlassen | to arrange, to settle |
| *abgemacht!* | *it's a bargain!* |
| *eine Abmachung treffen* | *to make an agreement* |
| **'ab\|nehmen** a-o/i (den Hut) → aufsetzen; → zunehmen (an Gewicht) | to take off (one's hat); to lose weight |
| **'ab\|reißen** i-i | to tear off; pull down |

| | |
|---|---|
| **der 'Abschied** s/e → Wiedersehen | leave-taking, departure |
| *sich verabschieden* | *to say good-bye* |
| *Abschied nehmen* | *to take leave* |
| **'ab\|schließen** o-o → aufschließen, öffnen | to lock |
| **die 'Absicht** /en | intention, purpose |
| *die Absicht haben (zu)* | *to intend (to)* |
| *in der besten Absicht* | *with the best intention* |
| *absichtlich* | *on purpose, intentionally* |
| **die Ab'teilung** /en | group, class; division; department |
| **'ab\|trocknen** | to wipe, to dry |
| **'abwärts** → aufwärts | down, downwards |
| **ach!** | Oh! |
| *ach so!* | *oh, I see!* |
| *ach was!* | *nonsense! not a bit! who cares!* |
| **'achten (auf)** | to respect; to pay attention to |
| **'acht\|geben** a-e/i **(auf)** | to look out for, to take care of |
| **die 'Achtung** | attention; respect |
| *aus Achtung vor* | *out of respect for* |
| **die A'dresse** /n | address |
| *adressieren (an)* | *to address (to)* |
| **'ähnlich** | similar to, (a)like |
| *das sieht ihm ähnlich* | *that's just like him* |
| *Ähnlichkeit haben (mit)* | *to be/look much like* |
| **das All** s | universe, cosmos |
| **'alle** → niemand | all; everybody |
| *alle Kinder* | *all the children* |
| *von allen Seiten* | *from all sides* |
| *alle beide* | *both of them* |
| *alle (zwei) Tage* | *every (other) day* |
| **al'lein** → zusammen | alone |
| *ganz allein* | *all alone* |
| *allein der Gedanke* | *the very thought of (it)* |

| | |
|---|---|
| *einzig und allein* | *simply, solely* |
| **der/die/das aller'beste** | the very best, the best of all |
| **aller'dings** | admittedly, of course |
| **'alles** → nichts | everything |
| *das ist alles* | *that's all* |
| *alles in allem* | *all in all* |
| *alles andere* | *everything else* |
| *Alles Gute!* | *All the best!* |
| *alles mögliche* | *all sorts of things* |
| **allge'mein** | general, usual |
| *im allgemeinen* | *in general, usually* |
| *die Allgemeinbildung* | *general education* |
| **'also** | so, consequently |
| **alt** → jung, neu | old; ancient; used; second-hand |
| *wie alt sind Sie?* | *what's your age?* |
| *sie ist 25 Jahre alt* | *she is 25 years old* |
| *wir sind gleich alt* | *we are the same age* |
| *alte Bücher* | *second-hand books* |
| *mein alter Lehrer* | *my former teacher* |
| *mein älterer Bruder* | *my elder brother* |
| *das alte Lied* | *the old story* |
| *er ist immer noch der alte* | *he ist still the same* |
| *alt werden* | *to grow old* |
| *alles bleibt beim alten* | *nothing has changed* |
| **der 'Alte** n/n | old man; boss |
| **das 'Alter** s/- | age; old age |
| *im Alter von* | *at the age of* |
| *er ist in meinem Alter* | *he is my age* |
| *das Mittelalter* | *Middle Ages* |
| *die Altersrente* | *old-age pension* |
| **A'merika** s | America |
| **der Ameri'kaner** s/- | American |
| *amerikanisch* | *American* |
| **das Amt** es/ä-er | office; post |
| **'an\|bieten** o-o | to offer |
| **der 'Anblick** s | sight, view, spectacle |

| | |
|---|---|
| *beim Anblick* | *at the sight of* |
| *beim ersten Anblick* | *at first sight* |
| *anblicken* | *to look at* |
| **der 'andere** → derselbe | the other |
| *ein anderer* | *another* |
| *die anderen* | *the others* |
| *andere* | *others* |
| *etwas anderes* | *something else* |
| *nichts anderes* | *nothing else* |
| *alles andere* | *everything else* |
| *unter anderem* | *among other things* |
| *einer nach dem andern* | *one after another, one at a time* |
| *einerseits . . . andrerseits* | *on the one hand . . . on the other hand* |
| **'ändern ; sich ändern** | to change |
| *daran läßt sich nichts ändern* | *that cannot be helped* |
| *seine Meinung ändern* | *to change o's mind* |
| *die Änderung* | *change* |
| **'anders** | otherwise |
| *jemand anders* | *somebody else* |
| *niemand anders (als)* | *nobody (else) but* |
| *ich kann nicht anders* | *I can't do otherwise* |
| **'anderswo(hin)** | elsewhere |
| **'an\|erkennen** a-a | to recognize |
| **der 'Anfang** s/ä-e → Ende | beginning, start |
| *am Anfang* | *in/at the beginning* |
| *von Anfang an* | *from the beginning* |
| *von Anfang bis Ende* | *from start to finish* |
| *Anfang Oktober* | *early in October* |
| **'an\|fangen** i-a/ä/beginnen (mit, zu) → aufhören | to begin, to start |
| **'anfangs** → zuletzt, schließlich | in the beginning, at first |
| **das 'Angebot** s/e → Nachfrage | offer |

| | |
|---|---|
| *ein Angebot machen* | *to make an offer* |
| *Angebot und Nachfrage* | *supply and demand* |
| **der 'Angeklagte** n/n | defendant, accused |
| **die 'Angelegenheit** /en | matter, business, affair |
| *kümmre dich um deine Angelegenheiten* | *mind your own business* |
| **'angenehm** → unangenehm | pleasant |
| **'an\|greifen** i-i → verteidigen | to attack; to take hold of |
| **der 'Angriff** s/e → Verteidigung | attack |
| *in Angriff nehmen* | *to start on, to set about* |
| **die Angst** /ä-e → Mut | anxiety, fear |
| *Angst haben (vor)* | *to be afraid (of)* |
| *mir ist angst* | *I'm afraid* |
| **'ängstlich** → mutig | anxious, fearful |
| **'an\|halten** ie-a/ä → weitergehen | to stop |
| *per Anhalter fahren* | *to hitch-hike* |
| **'an\|kommen** a-o → weggehen, abfahren | to arrive, to reach |
| *pünktlich ankommen* | *to arrive on time* |
| *mit 1 Stunde Verspätung ankommen* | *to be one hour late* |
| *das kommt darauf an!* | *that depends* |
| *er läßt es darauf ankommen* | *he'll take the chance* |
| *die Ankunft* | *arrival* |
| **'an\|machen** → ausmachen | to put on/switch on (the light) |
| **'an\|nehmen** a-o/i | to accept; to suppose |
| *mit Dank annehmen* | *to accept with thanks* |
| *ich nehme an, er ist krank* | *I suppose he is ill* |
| *nehmen wir an* | *let's suppose* |
| *angenommen . . .* | *assuming . . .* |
| **die 'Anordnung** /en | order, arrangement |
| **der 'Anruf** es/e | call |

| | |
|---|---|
| **'an\|rufen** ie-u | to call up/make a call/ ring up/give a ring |
| *nochmals anrufen* | *to ring again* |
| **'an\|sehen** a-e/ie | to look at |
| **die 'Ansicht** /en | opinion, view; sight |
| *meiner Ansicht nach* | *in my opinion* |
| **'anständig** → unanständig | decent, honest |
| *sei anständig!* | *behave yourself!* |
| *anständig behandeln* | *to give a square deal* |
| **die 'Antwort** /en → Frage | reply, answer |
| **'antworten (auf)** → fragen | to reply/answer, to make a reply/give an answer (to) |
| **'an\|wenden** a-a | to apply/use |
| **die 'Anwendung** /en | application, use |
| *Anwendung finden* | *to be used/put into practice* |
| **die 'Anzeige** /n | advertisement |
| *anzeigen* | *to advertise* |
| **'an\|ziehen** o-o | to put on, to dress; to attract |
| *den Mantel anziehen* | *to put on o's coat* |
| *sich anziehen* | *to dress* |
| *anziehend* | *attractive, interesting* |
| **der 'Anzug** s/ü-e | suit |
| *den Anzug anziehen* | *to put on o's suit* |
| **'an\|zünden** → auslöschen | to light |
| *das Feuer anzünden* | *to light the fire* |
| *ein Streichholz anzünden* | *to light/strike a match* |
| *eine Zigarre anzünden* | *to light a cigar* |
| **der 'Apfel** s/ä | apple |
| **die Apfel'sine** /n | orange |
| **die Apo'theke** /n | chemist's shop |
| **der Appa'rat** s/e | apparatus (telephone, camera, radio, etc). |
| *wer ist am Apparat?* | *who is speaking?* |
| *bleiben Sie am Apparat!* | *hold the line* |
| *der Fernsehapparat* | *television set* |

| | |
|---|---|
| *der Radioapparat* | *wireless set* |
| **die 'Arbeit** /en | work, labour |
| *an die Arbeit gehen, sich an die Arbeit machen* | *to go/set to work, to settle down to work* |
| *Arbeit suchen* | *to look for a job* |
| *der Arbeitgeber* | *employer* |
| *arbeitslos* | *out of work, unemployed* |
| *der Arbeitstag* | *working day* |
| **'arbeiten** | to work |
| *schwer arbeiten* | *to work hard* |
| **der 'Arbeiter** s/- | worker, workman |
| *der Facharbeiter* | *skilled worker* |
| **der Arm** s/e | arm |
| *den Arm brechen* | *to break o's arm* |
| *jdn mit offenen Armen aufnehmen* | *to welcome s.o. with open arms* |
| *die Armbanduhr* | *wrist-watch* |
| **arm**/ärmer/am ärmsten → reich | poor |
| *die Armen* pl | *the poor* pl |
| *die Armut* | *poverty* |
| **die Art** /en | manner, fashion, way; sort, kind |
| *auf diese Art und Weise* | *in this way* |
| *auf seine Art* | *in his way* |
| *auf deutsche Art* | *in the German way* |
| **der Ar'tikel** s/- | article |
| **die Arz'nei** /en | medicine |
| *die Arznei einnehmen* | *to take the medicine* |
| **der Arzt** es/ä-e | physician, doctor |
| *die Ärztin* | *lady doctor* |
| *den Arzt holen* | *to call in the doctor* |
| *zum Arzt gehen* | *to go to the doctor's* |
| *den Arzt rufen (lassen)* | *to send for the doctor* |
| **der Ast** es/ä-e | branch |
| **der 'Atem** s | breath |
| *außer Atem* | *out of breath* |
| *Atem holen* | *to take (a) breath* |

| | |
|---|---|
| *holen Sie tief Atem!* | *take a deep breath* |
| *atmen* | *to breathe* |
| **das A'tom** s/e | atom |
| *der Atomkrieg* | *atomic warfare* |
| *die Atomwaffen* pl | *atomic weapons* pl |
| **auch** | also, too |
| *ich auch nicht* | *neither do / am / have I* |
| **auf!** | come on!; get up! |
| *auf und ab* | *up and down; back and forth* |
| *er ist noch nicht auf* | *he isn't up yet* |
| *auf deutsch* | *in German* |
| **der 'Aufenthalt** s/e | stop, stay |
| **'auf\|fallen** ie-a/ä | to strike |
| *es fiel mir auf* | *I noticed* |
| *auffallend* | *striking, remarkable* |
| **die 'Aufgabe** /n | task; lesson, homework |
| *eine Aufgabe lösen* | *to solve a problem* |
| *seine Schulaufgaben machen* | *to do o's homework* |
| **'auf\|gehen** → untergehen | to rise |
| **'auf\|hängen** → abnehmen | to hang up |
| **'auf\|heben** o-o → hinlegen, weggeben | to pick up; to keep |
| **'auf\|hören** → anfangen | to stop, to break off |
| **'auf\|machen** | to open |
| **'aufmerksam** → unaufmerksam | attentive |
| *aufmerksam machen (auf)* | *to call attention* (*to*) |
| **die 'Aufmerksamkeit** /en → Unaufmerksamkeit | attention, regard |
| **die 'Aufnahme** /n | taking a picture; recording; photo |
| *Aufnahmen machen* | *to take pictures; to make recordings* |
| **'auf\|nehmen** a-o/i | to receive/welcome; to take pictures; to record |

| | |
|---|---|
| **'auf\|passen** | to pay attention; to look out, to mind |
| *aufgepaßt!* | *look out!* |
| **'auf\|stehen** a-a | to get up, to stand up |
| *aufstehen!* | *get up!* |
| **'auf\|stellen** | to set up, to arrange |
| *eine Liste aufstellen* | *to make out a list* |
| **der 'Auftrag** s/ä-e | order |
| *im Auftrag (i. A.)* | *on behalf of (p.p.)* |
| **'aufwärts** → abwärts | up, upwards |
| **das 'Auge** s/n | eye |
| *unter vier Augen* | *in private* |
| *mit bloßem Auge* | *with the naked eye* |
| *im Auge behalten* | *to keep in sight* |
| *aus den Augen verlieren* | *to lose sight of* |
| *große Augen machen* | *to open o's eyes wide* |
| **der Augen'blick** s/e | moment |
| *einen Augenblick, bitte* | *just a moment/minute, please* |
| *im Augenblick* | *at this moment, just now* |
| *er wird jeden Augenblick hier sein* | *he'll be here at any moment* |
| *augenblicklich* | *this minute* |
| **aus, es ist aus** | it's finished |
| *ein . . . aus* | *on . . . off* |
| **die 'Ausbildung** | education, training |
| **der 'Ausdruck** s/ü-e | expression |
| *ausdrücken* | *to express* |
| **die 'Ausfahrt** /en → Einfahrt | exit, way out |
| *Ausfahrt freilassen* | *No parking in front of these gates* |
| **'aus\|führen** → einführen | to carry out; to export |
| **der 'Ausgang** s/ä-e → Eingang | way out, exit |
| *Notausgang* | *Emergency exit* |
| *Kein Ausgang* | *No exit* |
| **'aus\|geben** → einnehmen | to spend |

| | |
|---|---|
| **'ausgeschlossen** | out of the question |
| **'aus\|halten** ie-a/ä | to suffer/bear/stand |
| *ich halte es nicht mehr aus* | *I can't stand it any longer* |
| **die 'Auskunft** /ü-e | information |
| **das 'Ausland** s → Inland | foreign countries |
| *im/ins Ausland* | *abroad* |
| *ins Ausland gehen* | *to go abroad* |
| *der Ausländer* | *foreigner* |
| *ausländisch* | *foreign* |
| **'aus\|löschen, 'ausmachen** → anzünden | to put out/switch off |
| **die 'Ausnahme** /n → Regel | exception |
| *mit Ausnahme von* | *except(ing), with the exception of* |
| **'aus\|rufen** ie-u | to call out, to exclaim |
| **'aus\|ruhen, sich ausruhen** | to rest, to take a rest |
| **'aus\|schalten** → einschalten | to switch/turn off |
| **'aus\|sehen** a-e/ie | to look; to appear |
| *gut/schlecht aussehen* | *to look well/unwell* |
| *er sieht aus wie . . .* | *he looks like . . .* |
| *er sieht krank aus* | *he looks ill* |
| *es sieht nach Regen aus* | *it looks like rain* |
| **'außen** → innen | outside |
| *von außen* | *from (the) outside* |
| *die Außenseite* | *outside* |
| **'außerdem** | besides, moreover, what is more |
| **'äußere** → innere | exterior |
| **'außergewöhnlich** → gewöhnlich | extraordinary, special |
| **'äußerst** | extreme(ly) |
| *im äußersten Fall* | *at the worst* |
| **die 'Aussicht** /en | view; chance |
| **'aus\|sprechen** a-o/i | to pronounce |
| **'aus\|steigen** ie-ie → einsteigen | to get off/out |

| | |
|---|---|
| *steigen Sie aus?* | *are you getting off?* |
| **die 'Ausstellung** /en | show, fair, exhibition |
| *das Ausstellungsgelände* | *exhibition grounds* |
| *ausgestellt sein* | *to be on display* |
| **der 'Ausweis** es/e | pass, identity card |
| *die Ausweispapiere* | *identity papers* |
| **'auswendig** | by heart |
| *auswendig lernen* | *to learn by heart* |
| **'aus\|wischen** | to wipe out |
| **'aus\|ziehen** o-o → anziehen | to take off |
| *sich ausziehen* | *to undress* |
| **das 'Auto** s/s | (motor-)car |
| *mit dem Auto fahren* | *to go by car* |
| *Auto fahren* | *to drive (a car)* |
| *die Autobahn* | *motorway* |
| *der Autofahrer* | *motorist* |

## B

| | |
|---|---|
| **'backen** u-a/ä | to bake |
| *der Bäcker* | *baker* |
| **das Bad** es/ä-er | bath; bathe; bathroom |
| *ein Bad nehmen* | *to take a bath* |
| **'baden** | to bath/bathe; to take a bath; to have a bathe |
| **die Bahn** /en | railway |
| *mit der Bahn fahren* | *to go by train* |
| *der Bahnhof* | *station* |
| *der Bahnsteig* | *platform* |
| **bald** | soon; early |
| *auf bald!* | *so long!* |
| *so bald wie möglich* | *as soon as possible* |
| **der Ball** s/ä-e | ball |
| *Ball spielen* | *to play ball* |
| **die Ba'nane** /n | banana |

| | |
|---|---|
| **das Band** es/ä-er | ribbon, band |
| **der Band** s/ä-e | volume |
| **die Bank** /ä-e; /en | bench; bank |
| **'basteln** | to rig up; to do odd jobs |
| **der Bau** s/ten | building |
| *bauen* | *to build* |
| **der Bauch** s/äu-e | belly, abdomen |
| **der 'Bauer** n/n | peasant, farmer |
| *der Bauernhof* | *farm* |
| **der Baum** es/äu-e | tree |
| *auf einen Baum **klettern*** | *to climb (up) **a tree*** |
| **der Be'amte** n/n | official, civil servant |
| **der Be'darf** s | need, want |
| *Bedarf haben* | *to be in need (of), to want* |
| *den Bedarf decken* | *to supply the need* |
| **be'dauern** | to regret |
| *zu meinem (großen) Bedauern* | *(much) to my regret* |
| **be'decken (mit)** | to cover (with) |
| **be'deuten** | to mean |
| *bedeutend* | *important, great* |
| **die Be'deutung** /en | meaning; importance |
| **be'dienen** | to serve, to wait on |
| *sich bedienen* | *to help o.s.* |
| *bedienen Sie sich!* | *help yourself* |
| **die Be'dingung** /en | condition |
| *unter der Bedingung, daß* | *on condition that* |
| *unter einer Bedingung* | *on one condition* |
| *unter welchen Bedingungen?* | *on what conditions?* |
| *zu günstigen Bedingungen* | *on easy terms* |
| **be'enden** → beginnen | to finish, to end |
| **der Be'fehl** s/e | order |
| **be'fehlen** a-o → gehorchen | to order |
| **be'gegnen** / treffen | to meet |
| *die Begegnung* | *meeting* |

| | |
|---|---|
| **der Be'ginn** s → Ende / Schluß | beginning |
| *zu Beginn* | *at the beginning (of)* |
| *Beginn der Vorstellung (um) ...* | *the curtain goes up (at)* |
| **be'ginnen** a-o → beenden / aufhören | to begin, to set in, to start |
| **be'gleiten** | to accompany/go with |
| *jdn nach Hause begleiten* | *to see s.o. home* |
| *der Begleiter* | *companion* |
| *die Begleitung* | *company* |
| *in Begleitung von* | *accompanied by* |
| **der Be'griff** s/e | idea |
| *im Begriff sein* | *to be going to* |
| **be'halten** ie-a/ä → wegschaffen | to keep |
| *behalte das für dich* | *keep this private* |
| **be'handeln** | to treat, to attend |
| *einen Kranken behandeln* | *to treat a patient* |
| *anständig behandeln* | *to give a square deal* |
| *die Behandlung* | *treatment, care* |
| **be'haupten** | to maintain, to state |
| *die Behauptung* | *statement* |
| **die Be'hörde** /n | authority/ies |
| **'beide** | both |
| *alle beide* | *both of them* |
| *keiner von beiden* | *neither (of the two)* |
| *auf beiden Seiten* | *on both sides* |
| **das Bein** s/e | leg |
| *das Bein brechen* | *to break o's leg* |
| *auf den Beinen sein* | *to be on the move* |
| *das Tischbein* | *table leg* |
| **'beinahe** / fast | almost, nearly |
| **das 'Beispiel** s/e | example, instance |
| *zum Beispiel (z.B.)* | *for example/for instance (e.g.)* |
| *wie zum Beispiel* | *such as* |
| *ein Beispiel geben* | *to set an example* |

| | |
|---|---|
| **'beißen** i-i | to bite |
| *in den sauren Apfel beißen* | *to swallow the bitter pill* |
| **be'kannt** → unbekannt / | (well-)known, familiar |
| *mit jdm bekannt sein* | *to be acquainted with s.o.* |
| *es ist bekannt, daß* | *it's (generally) known that* |
| **der Be'kannte** n/n → Unbekannte / Fremde | acquaintance |
| *ein (guter) Bekannter von mir* | *a friend of mine* |
| **die Be'kanntmachung** /en | notice |
| **be'kommen** a-o → geben | to receive, to get |
| **be'laden** u-a/ä → abladen | to load |
| **be'liebt** → unbeliebt | popular |
| **be'lohnen** → bestrafen | to reward |
| *die Belohnung* | *reward* |
| **be'merken** | to remark; to notice |
| *bemerkenswert* | *remarkable* |
| **sich be'mühen** | to try, to take trouble |
| *die Bemühung* | *effort, trouble* |
| **sich be'nehmen** a-o/i | to behave |
| *sich anständig benehmen* | *to behave properly* |
| **be'nutzen** | to use |
| *den Zug benutzen* | *to go by train* |
| **das Ben'zin** s/e | petrol, gas(oline) *am* |
| **be'obachten** | to observe |
| *die Beobachtung* | *observation* |
| **be'quem** → unbequem | comfortable; at ease, easy |
| *machen Sie sich's bequem* | *make yourself comfortable* |
| **be'reit** | ready |
| *sich bereit machen* | *to make o.s. ready* |
| *bereit sein zu* | *to be prepared to* |
| **be'reits** / schon | already |
| **der Berg** es/e → Tal | mountain |
| *einen Berg besteigen* | *to climb a mountain* |
| *über Berg und Tal* | *over hill and dale* |

| | |
|---|---|
| **der Be'richt** s/e | report, account |
| **be'richten** | to report, to tell |
| **der Be'ruf** es/e | profession, trade, occupation |
| *von Beruf* | *by profession/trade* |
| *einen Beruf ergreifen* | *to enter a profession* |
| *einen Beruf ausüben* | *to practise a profession* |
| *beruflich* | *professional* |
| **be'rühmt** | famous |
| **be'rühren** | to touch |
| *bitte nicht berühren!* | *please do not touch* |
| *die Berührung* | *touch* |
| **be'schäftigen** | to employ, to occupy |
| *sich mit etwas beschäftigen* | *to be busy with* |
| *beschäftigt sein* | *to be occupied* |
| **be'schließen** o-o | to determine |
| **der Be'schluß** sses/üsse | decision, resolution |
| **der 'Besen** s/- | broom |
| **be'setzen** | to occupy |
| *besetzt* | *engaged; full up* |
| **der Be'sitz** es/Besitztümer / Besitzungen | property, possession |
| *in Besitz nehmen* | *to take possession of* |
| **be'sitzen** a-e | to possess/own/have (got) |
| **be'sondere(r,s)** | special, particular |
| *nichts Besonderes* | *nothing unusual* |
| **be'sonders** | particularly, especially |
| **be'sorgen** | to see to; to get |
| *Besorgungen machen* | *to run errands* |
| **'besser** (cf. **gut**) | better |
| *immer besser* | *better and better* |
| *desto besser!* | *so much the better* |
| *etwas Besseres* | *something better* |
| *am besten* | *best* |
| *der (die, das) beste* | *the best* |
| *das Beste* | *the best (thing)* |
| *er tut sein Bestes* | *he does his best* |

| | |
|---|---|
| *ich danke bestens* | *thank you very much* |
| **be'stehen** a-a **(aus)** | to consist (of), to be composed (of) |
| *eine Prüfung bestehen* | *to pass an examination* |
| **be'stellen** | to order, to ask, to give an order |
| *ein Bier bestellen* | *to order a beer* |
| *2 Plätze bestellen* | *to book 2 seats* |
| *schöne Grüße bestellen* | *to send kind regards* |
| **be'stimmen** | to determine; to set |
| **be'stimmt** → unbestimmt / vielleicht | for sure, certainly, without doubt |
| *er kommt bestimmt* | *he is sure to come* |
| **be'strafen (für)** → belohnen | to punish (for) |
| **der Be'such** s/e | visit |
| *jdm einen Besuch machen* | *to pay s.o. a visit* |
| *auf Besuch (bei)* | *on a visit (to)* |
| *Besuch haben* | *to have visitors* |
| **be'suchen** | to visit; to go/come to see |
| *besuche mich einmal* | *come to see me sometime* |
| *das Theater besuchen* | *to go to the theatre* |
| **be'trachten** / ansehen | to regard; to view |
| *das kommt nicht in Betracht* | *that's out of the question* |
| *beträchtlich* | *considerable* |
| **der Be'trag** s/ä-e | sum, amount |
| *Betrag erhalten* | *payment received* |
| *betragen* | *to amount to* |
| *der Preis beträgt 3 DM* | *the price is 3 marks* |
| **be'treffen** a-o/i | to concern |
| *was mich betrifft* | *as for me* |
| **be'treten** a-e/i → verlassen | to enter |
| *Betreten verboten!* | *Keep off! No entrance* |
| **der Be'trieb** s/e | works, (work)shop, factory |

| | |
|---|---|
| *außer Betrieb* | *out of action / order* |
| *in Betrieb* | *in action / operation* |
| *in Betrieb setzen* | *to put into operation* |
| **das Bett** s/en | bed |
| *zu Bett gehen* | *to go to bed* |
| *das Bett hüten* | *to stay in bed* |
| *noch im Bett* | *still in bed* |
| *die Bettwäsche* | *bed linen* |
| **be'urteilen** | to judge |
| **die Be'völkerung** | population |
| **be'wegen** | to move |
| *sich bewegen* | *to move* |
| *die Bewegung* | *movement* |
| **der Be'weis es/e** | proof, argument |
| *beweisen* | *to prove, to argue* |
| **das Be'wußtsein** s | consciousness |
| *das Bewußtsein verlieren* | *to lose consciousness* |
| **be'zahlen** | to pay |
| *teuer bezahlen* | *to pay dear* (*for*) |
| *die Bezahlung* | *pay*(*ment*) |
| *gegen Bezahlung* | *against payment* |
| **be'zeichnen** | to mark; to characterize |
| *bezeichnend* | *representative* |
| **die Be'ziehung** /en | regard, relation |
| *in dieser Beziehung* | *in this regard* |
| *in jeder Beziehung* | *in every regard* |
| *beziehungsweise* | *and . . . respectively; or* |
| **das Bier** s/e | beer |
| **'bieten** o-o | offer, present |
| **das Bild** s/er | picture; image; painting; photo |
| *der Bildschirm* | (*television*) *screen* |
| **'bilden** | to form; to educate |
| *ein gebildeter Mensch* | *a cultured person* |
| *die Bildung* | *formation; education* |
| *die Allgemeinbildung* | *general education* |
| **'billig** → teuer | cheap |

| | |
|---|---|
| **bin** (1st pers sg pres of **sein**) | |
| **'binden** a-u → lösen | to bind, to tie |
| *der Bindfaden* | *string* |
| **die 'Birne** /n | pear |
| **bis dann** | till then |
| *bis dahin* | *by then* |
| *bis jetzt* | *up to now, as yet* |
| *bis morgen!* | *see you tomorrow!* |
| **bis'her** | till now, as yet |
| **ein 'bißchen** → viel | a little, a (little) bit |
| **bist** (2nd pers sg pres of **sein**) | |
| **'bitte!** → danke! | please; don't mention it, you are welcome |
| *bitte?* | *pardon?* |
| *wie bitte?* | *I beg your pardon?* |
| **die 'Bitte** /n → Dank | request |
| **'bitten** a-e → danken | to request/ask/beg |
| *darf ich Sie bitten?* | *may I trouble you?* |
| *(ich bitte um) Verzeihung!* | *(I beg your) pardon; sorry!* |
| **'bitter** | bitter |
| **das Blatt** es/ä-er | leaf |
| *ein Blatt Papier* | *a sheet of paper* |
| **blau** | blue |
| *hellblau/dunkelblau* | *light blue/dark blue* |
| **'bleiben** ie-ie → weggehen, sich ändern | to stay, to remain |
| *zu Hause bleiben* | *to stay in* |
| *es bleibt dabei* | *agreed* |
| *bleiben Sie sitzen!* | *please remain seated, don't get up* |
| *es bleiben zwei übrig* | *there are two left* |
| **der 'Bleistift** s/e | pencil |
| **der Blick** s/e | look; view |
| *auf den ersten Blick* | *at first sight* |
| *einen Blick werfen (auf)* | *to take a look (at)* |

| | |
|---|---|
| *blicken* | *to look* |
| **blind** → sehend | blind |
| der **Blitz** es/e | lightning, flash |
| *es blitzt* | *it is lightening* |
| **bloß**/nur | only, simply |
| *der bloße Gedanke an* | *the very thought of* |
| '**blühen** | to bloom |
| *die Blüte* | *flower, blossom* |
| *in Blüte stehen* | *to be in(full) bloom* |
| die '**Blume** /n | flower |
| die '**Bluse** /n | blouse |
| das **Blut** es | blood |
| *bluten* | *to bleed* |
| der '**Boden** s/ö | soil, ground; floor; bottom |
| *auf dem Boden* | *on the ground* |
| der **Bord** s/e | board |
| *an Bord gehen* | *to go on board* |
| *an Bord* | *aboard* |
| '**böse** | evil; angry |
| *jdm böse sein* | *to be angry with s.o.* |
| *böse werden* | *to get angry* |
| '**braten** | to roast |
| '**brauchen** | to need, to require, to want |
| *er braucht Geld* | *he needs money* |
| **braun** | brown |
| *die Braunkohle* | *brown/soft coal, lignite* |
| '**brechen** a-o/i | to break |
| *den Arm brechen* | *to break o's arm* |
| *sein Wort brechen* | *to break o's word* |
| **breit** → eng, schmal | broad, wide |
| *4 Meter breit sein* | *to be 4 metres wide* |
| *wie breit ist . . .?* | *how wide is . . .?* |
| *die Breite* | *breadth* |
| '**brennen** a-a | to burn; to be on fire |
| *es brennt!* | *fire!* |
| *das Haus brennt* | *the house is on fire* |

| | |
|---|---|
| *wo brennt's denn?* | *what's the matter?* |
| **das Brett** es/er | board |
| *das Bücherbrett* | *bookshelf* |
| **der Brief** es/e | letter |
| *Briefe wechseln (mit)* | *to correspond (with)* |
| *eingeschriebener Brief* | *registered letter* |
| *einen Brief freimachen* | *to stamp a letter* |
| *einen Brief zur Post bringen* | *to post a letter* |
| *einen Brief erhalten* | *to get a letter* |
| *der Briefkasten* | *letter-box, pillar-box* |
| *die Briefmarke* | *stamp* |
| *Briefmarken sammeln* | *to collect stamps* |
| *das Briefpapier* | *note paper* |
| *der Briefträger* | *postman* |
| *der Briefumschlag* | *envelope* |
| **die 'Brille** /n | glasses *pl* |
| *eine Brille tragen* | *to wear glasses* |
| *die Brille aufsetzen* | *to put on o's glasses* |
| **'bringen** a-a | to bring; to take |
| *Hilfe bringen* | *to bring help* |
| *Glück bringen* | *to bring good luck* |
| *Gewinn bringen* | *to yield a profit* |
| **das Brot** es/e | bread, loaf of bread |
| *sein Brot verdienen* | *to earn one's livelihood* |
| *das Brötchen* | *roll* |
| *eine Scheibe Brot* | *a slice of bread* |
| *ein Stück Brot* | *a piece of bread* |
| **die 'Brücke** /n | bridge |
| **der 'Bruder** s/ü | brother |
| *mein älterer Bruder* | *my elder brother* |
| *mein jüngerer Bruder* | *my younger brother* |
| **die Brust** /ü-e | chest; breast |
| **das Buch** s/ü-er | book |
| *das antiquarische Buch* | *second-hand book* |
| *die Bücherei* | *library* |
| **der 'Buchstabe** n/n | letter, character |
| *buchstabieren* | *to spell* |
| **'bügeln** | to iron |

| | |
|---|---|
| **die 'Bühne /n** | scene, stage |
| **bunt** | coloured; multi-coloured |
| **der 'Bürger s/-** | citizen |
| **das Bü'ro s/s** | office |
| **die 'Bürste /n** | brush |
| *bürsten* | *to brush* |
| **der Bus ses/se** | bus; coach |
| *mit dem Bus fahren* | *to go by bus* |
| *die Bushaltestelle* | *bus stop* |
| **die 'Butter** | butter |

## C

| | |
|---|---|
| **der Cha'rakter** s/e | character |
| **der Chef** s/s | chief, head |
| **die Che'mie** | chemistry |
| *chemisch* | *chemical* |
| **der Chor** s/ö-e | choir, chorus |

## D

| | |
|---|---|
| **da** → hier / fort / weg | (over) there; then; present |
| *da!* | *look!* |
| *hier und da* | *here and there* |
| *da ist / sind* | *there is/are* |
| *da haben wir's* | *there we are* |
| *da bin ich* | *here I am* |
| **da'bei** | there, present |
| *ich war dabei* | *I was there* |
| *gerade dabei sein zu* | *to be about to* |
| **das Dach** s/ä-er | roof |
| **'dachte** (1st, 3rd pers sg pret of **denken**) | |

| | |
|---|---|
| **'dadurch** | through there; by this means |
| **dafür** | for it; instead (of) |
| *'dafür danke ich Ihnen* | *I thank you for it* |
| *ich kann nichts da'für* | *I can't help it* |
| **da'gegen** | against it; on the other hand, on the contrary |
| *ich habe nichts dagegen* | *I don't mind (it)* |
| *wenn Sie nichts dagegen haben* | *if you don't object* |
| **'daher** | so; therefore |
| *daher kommt es, daß* | *thus it happens that* |
| **'dahin** | (over) there |
| *bis dahin* | *until then, so far* |
| **da'hin** | gone |
| **da'hinter** → davor | behind |
| **'damals** | then, at that time |
| **die 'Dame** /n | lady |
| *meine Damen und Herren!* | *ladies and gentlemen* |
| *Damen – Herren/D–H* | *Ladies – Gentlemen* |
| **'damit** | with that/it |
| *was meinen Sie damit?* | *what do you mean by it?* |
| **der Dampf** es/ä-e | steam |
| *mit Volldampf* | *full steam ahead* |
| *der Dampfer* | *steamer, liner* |
| **da'nach** | afterwards; accordingly |
| *gleich danach* | *soon after* |
| **da'neben** | near it |
| *gleich daneben* | *close by* |
| **der Dank** es → Bitte | thanks *pl* |
| *vielen Dank!* | *many thanks* |
| *mit Dank annehmen* | *to accept with thanks* |
| *dankbar* | *grateful* |
| *danke!* | *thank you* |
| *danke sehr!* | *thank you very much* |
| *danke, gleichfalls* | *thank you, the same to you* |
| **'danken** (jdm für etw) → bitten | to thank (s.o. for sth.) |

| | |
|---|---|
| *nichts zu danken!* | *don't mention it* |
| *ja, danke!* | *thank you!* |
| *danke, nein!* | *no, thank you* |
| **dann** | then |
| *und dann?* | *and what then?* |
| *dann und wann* | *now and again* |
| **da'ran** | at that/it |
| *wer ist dran?* | *whose turn is it?* |
| *nahe daran sein (zu)* | *to be on the point (of)* |
| *sich daran machen* | *to set to* |
| **da'rauf** → darunter | on that/it; afterwards |
| **da'raus** | out of that/it |
| **da'rin** | in that/it |
| **darf** (1st, 3rd pers sg pres of **dürfen**) | |
| **'dar\|legen** | to explain, state |
| **'dar\|stellen** | to picture; to represent |
| **da'rüber** → darunter | over that/it; about that |
| *'darüber hinaus* | *beyond it* |
| **'darum** | that's why |
| **da'runter** → darauf, darüber | under that/it |
| **das** | this; that |
| *das, was* | *what* |
| **'da\|sein** | to exist; to be present |
| *das Dasein* | *existence, being* |
| **dasselbe** | the same thing |
| **'dauern** | to last |
| *lange dauern* | *to take a long time* |
| *dauernd* | *permanent; constant* |
| **der 'Daumen** s/- | thumb |
| **davon** | of that/it; away |
| *er ist auf und da'von* | *he's run away* |
| *'davon weiß ich nichts* | *I know nothing about it* |
| **'dazu** | to that/it; therefore; besides |
| *dazu kommt* | *add to this* |

| | |
|---|---|
| **die 'Decke /n** | cover, cloth; ceiling; layer |
| **der 'Deckel s/-** | lid |
| **'decken** | to cover |
| *den Bedarf decken* | *to supply the need* |
| *den Tisch decken* | *to lay the table* |
| **'denken** a-a **(an)** | to think (of) |
| *wo denken Sie hin!* | *not on your life!* |
| *denken Sie mal!* | *just imagine! think of it!* |
| *ja, ich denke schon* | *I think so* |
| **'dennoch** | however, anyhow, all the same |
| **der'selbe** → der andere | the same |
| **'deshalb** | therefore, that is why, for that reason |
| **'desto** | (so much) the |
| *je eher, desto besser!* | *the sooner the better* |
| *desto schlimmer!* | *so much the worse* |
| **'deswegen** | that's why |
| eben deswegen | *for that very reason* |
| **'deutlich** → undeutlich | distinct |
| **deutsch** | German |
| *auf deutsch* | *in German* |
| *deutsch sprechen* | *to speak German* |
| *ich lerne Deutsch* | *I learn German* |
| *ins Deutsche übersetzen* | *to translate into German* |
| *sprechen Sie Deutsch?* | *do you speak German?* |
| *er versteht Deutsch* | *he understands German* |
| **der 'Deutsche** n/n | German |
| *wir Deutschen* | *we Germans* |
| **'Deutschland** s | Germany |
| *in/nach Deutschland* | *in/to Germany* |
| **dicht** | dense; thick; tight |
| *dicht bei* | *close by* |
| *dicht aneinander* | *close together* |
| **der 'Dichter** s/- | poet |
| *die Dichtung* | *fiction* |

| | |
|---|---|
| **dick** → dünn | thick, fat |
| *2 Meter dick* | *2 metres thick* |
| **der Dieb** s/e | thief |
| *haltet den Dieb!* | *stop thief!* |
| **'dienen** → herrschen | to serve |
| *womit kann ich dienen?* | *what can I do for you?* |
| **der Dienst** es/e | service; office |
| *Dienst haben* | *to be on duty* |
| *dienstfrei haben* | *to be off duty* |
| *einen Dienst erweisen* | *to render a service* |
| **dies** | this |
| **'diese(r,s)** → jener | this/this one |
| **'diesmal** | this once/time |
| **das Ding** es/e; / Sache | thing |
| *vor allen Dingen* | *first of all* |
| **di'rekt** → indirekt | directly |
| **der Di'rektor** s/en | director; headmaster |
| **doch** | still, after all |
| *komm doch!* | *do come!* |
| *doch, ich komme* | *yes, I'm coming, I'll come* |
| *ja doch!* | *yes, indeed!* |
| *nicht doch!* | *don't!* |
| **der 'Doktor** s/en | doctor |
| *Herr Doktor!* | *doctor* |
| *den Doktor holen* | *to send for the doctor* |
| **der 'Donner** s | thunder |
| *ein Donnerschlag* | *a clap of thunder* |
| *es donnert* | *it's thundering* |
| **'doppelt** | double, twice |
| **das Dorf** s/ö-er | village |
| **dort** → hier | (over) there |
| *wer ist dort?* | *who is speaking?* |
| **'dorthin** → hierher | there |
| **der Draht** es/ä-er | wire |
| *drahtlos* | *wireless* |
| **dran** (cf. **daran**) | |
| *wer ist dran?* | *whose turn is it?* |

| | |
|---|---|
| *Sie sind dran* | *it's your turn* |
| **'drängen** | to press |
| *nicht drängen!* | *don't push* |
| **drauf** (cf. **darauf**) | |
| **'draußen** → darin | outside, out of doors |
| **'drehen** | to turn |
| **drin** (cf. **darin**) | |
| **'dringend** | urgent |
| *die Sache ist dringend* | *the matter is urgent* |
| **'drinnen** | inside; within; in (it) |
| **'drohen** | to threaten |
| **'drüben** | on the other side |
| **der Druck** s/ü-e; u-e | pressure; print |
| **'drucken** | to print |
| **'drücken** | to press |
| *den Knopf drücken* | *to press the button* |
| *die Hand drücken* | *to shake hands (with)* |
| *Drücken!* | *Push* |
| **dumm** → klug / weise | stupid, silly |
| *dummes Zeug reden* | *to talk nonsense* |
| *eine Dummheit machen* | *to do a silly thing* |
| *mach keine Dummheiten* | *don't do anything silly* |
| *der Dummkopf* | *ass, fool* |
| **'dunkel** → hell | dark; obscure |
| *im Dunkeln* | *in the dark* |
| *es ist dunkel* | *it is dark* |
| *es wird dunkel* | *it's getting dark* |
| *dunkelblau* | *dark blue* |
| *die Dunkelheit* | *darkness* |
| *bei einbrechender Dunkelheit* | *at nightfall/dusk* |
| **dünn** → dick | fine, thin |
| **durch und durch** | thoroughly |
| *durch und durch naß* | *wet through* |
| **durch'aus** | quite, absolutely |
| *durch'aus nicht!* | *not at all, by no means* |
| **durchein'ander** | in disorder |

| | |
|---|---|
| *ich bin ganz durcheinander* | *I'm all mixed up* |
| **die 'Durchfahrt** /en | passage |
| *Durchfahrt verboten!* | *No thoroughfare* |
| **'durch\|führen** | to carry out, to execute |
| **durch'queren** | to cross |
| **der 'Durchschnitt** s/e | average |
| *im Durchschnitt / durchschnittlich* | *on an average* |
| *über dem Durchschnitt* | *above average* |
| *unter dem Durchschnitt* | *below average* |
| **'durch\|sehen** a-e/ie | to look through |
| **'dürfen** u-u/a | to be allowed/permitted |
| *Sie dürfen gehen* | *you may go* |
| **der Durst** es | thirst |
| *Durst haben* | *to be thirsty* |
| *durstig* | *thirsty* |
| **'duschen** | to take a shower(-bath) |
| **das 'Dutzend** s/e | dozen |
| *dutzendweise* | *by the dozen* |

## E

| | |
|---|---|
| **'eben** → uneben | even |
| *die Ebene* | *plain; level* |
| **'eben** | just (now) |
| *eben!* | *exactly!* |
| *er ist eben weggegangen* | *he has just left* |
| **'ebenfalls** / auch | also, as well, too |
| *danke, ebenfalls!* | *thank you, the same to you* |
| **'ebenso** | alike, as well |
| *ebenso . . . wie* | *as . . . as* |
| *ebenso gut wie* | *as well as* |
| *ebenso viel/e wie* | *as much/many as* |
| **echt** → falsch | true; real, pure |
| *das ist echt!* | *that's typical* |
| **die 'Ecke** /n | corner |

| | |
|---|---|
| *an der Ecke* | *at the (street) corner* |
| *in der Ecke* | *in the corner* |
| *um die Ecke biegen* | *to turn the corner* |
| **e'gal / gleich** | equal |
| *das ist mir egal* | *I don't care, it's all the same (to me)* |
| **die 'Ehe /n** | marriage |
| **'eher** | rather |
| **die 'Ehre /n** | honour |
| *zu Ehren von* | *in honour of* |
| *ehren* | *to honour* |
| *Sehr geehrter Herr* | *(Dear) Sir* |
| **das Ei s/er** | egg |
| *ein weiches Ei* | *a soft-boiled egg* |
| *ein hartes Ei* | *a hard-boiled egg* |
| *ein Ei kochen* | *to boil an egg* |
| *Rührei* | *scrambled eggs* |
| *Spiegelei(er)* | *fried egg(s)* |
| **'eigen** → fremd | own |
| *mit eigenen Augen* | *with o's own eyes* |
| *einen eigenen Wagen haben* | *to have a car of o's own* |
| **die 'Eigenschaft /en** | property; quality |
| **'eigentlich** | to tell the truth; really |
| *was willst du eigentlich?* | *what do you want anyhow?* |
| **das 'Eigentum s/ü-er** | property |
| **die 'Eile** | haste |
| *in aller Eile* | *in great haste* |
| *in Eile sein* | *to be in a rush* |
| *eilen, sich beeilen* | *to make haste, to hurry* |
| *es eilt* | *it's urgent* |
| *ich habe es eilig* | *I'm in a hurry* |
| **der 'Eimer s/-** | pail, bucket |
| **ein . . . aus** | on . . . off |
| **ein'ander** | each other, one another |
| **der 'Eindruck s/ü-e** | impression |
| *Eindruck machen* | *to impress, to make an impression* |

| | |
|---|---|
| **'einfach** | simple; plain |
| *einfach, zweiter (Klasse)* | *second (class), single* |
| **die 'Einfahrt /en** → Ausfahrt | entrance |
| *Einfahrt verboten!* | *No entry* |
| *Einfahrt frei halten!* | *Do not obstruct this entrance* |
| **der 'Einfluß sses/üsse** | influence |
| *Einfluß ausüben (auf)* | *to exercise an influence (on)* |
| **'ein\|führen** | to introduce; to import |
| **der 'Eingang** s/ä-e → Ausgang | entrance, way in |
| *Eingang verboten!* | *No entry* |
| **'einige** → alle / sämtliche | some, a few |
| **'ein\|kaufen** → verkaufen | to shop/go shopping, to do the shopping |
| *billig / teuer einkaufen* | *to buy cheap/dear* |
| **'ein\|laden** u-a/ä | to invite, ask |
| *die Einladung* | *invitation* |
| *einer Einladung folgen* | *to accept an invitation* |
| **'einmal** | once |
| *noch einmal* | *once more* |
| *auf einmal* | *suddenly* |
| *ein für allemal* | *once and for all* |
| *es war einmal* | *once upon a time* |
| *nicht einmal* | *not even* |
| *hör einmal* | *listen!* |
| **'ein\|richten** | to arrange; to install; to establish |
| *schön eingerichtet* | *well-furnished* |
| *es einrichten, daß* | *to see to it that* |
| **'ein\|schalten** → ausschalten | to switch on; to turn on |
| **einst** | once |
| **'ein\|steigen** ie-ie → aussteigen | to get in, into |
| *einsteigen, bitte!* | *all aboard!* |

| | |
|---|---|
| **'ein\|stellen** | to regulate, to set |
| **'ein\|treten** a-e/i (in) | to enter, to get in, to come in |
| **der 'Eintritt** s | entrance, admission |
| *Eintritt frei!* | *Entrance free* |
| *Eintritt verboten!* | *Keep out. No admittance* |
| *die Eintrittskarte* | *ticket* |
| *eine Eintrittskarte lösen* | *to buy a ticket* |
| **'einverstanden** | agreed, all right |
| *(mit etwas) einverstanden sein* | *to agree* (*to sth.*) |
| **die 'Einzelheit** /en | detail |
| *in allen Einzelheiten* | *in detail* |
| **'einzeln** → zusammen | single; one by one |
| *ins einzelne gehen* | *to go into details* |
| **'einzig** | single, only |
| *einzig und allein* | *solely* |
| **das Eis** es | ice; ice-cream |
| **das 'Eisen** s/- | iron |
| *die Eisenindustrie* | *iron industry* |
| *die Eisenbahn* | *railway* |
| *mit der Eisenbahn* | *by rail/train* |
| **e'lektrisch** | electric(al) |
| *der elektrische Strom* | *electric current* |
| *der Elektriker* | *electrician* |
| *die Elektrizität* | *electricity* |
| **die 'Eltern** pl | parents |
| **emp'fangen** i-a/ä | to receive |
| **emp'finden** a-u | to sense, to feel |
| **das 'Ende** s/n → Anfang | end |
| *am Ende* | *at/in the end* |
| *zu Ende* | *at an end* |
| *am Ende der Straße* | *at the end of the street* |
| *zu Ende gehen* | *to come to an end* |
| *ein Ende machen* | *to put an end to* |
| *Ende Mai* | *at the end of May* |
| **'enden** → anfangen | to end, to bring to an end |

| | |
|---|---|
| **'endlich** | at last, finally |
| **eng** → weit | tight, narrow |
| *eng verbunden* | *closely allied* |
| **'England** s | England; Great Britain |
| **der 'Engländer** s/- | Englishman |
| **'englisch** | English |
| *die englische Sprache* | *the English language* |
| *auf englisch* | *in English* |
| *er kann Englisch* | *he speaks English* |
| **ent'decken** | to discover |
| *die Entdeckung* | *discovery* |
| **ent'fernt** → nahe | away, (far) off, distant |
| *2 Kilometer entfernt* | *2 kilometres off/away* |
| **die Ent'fernung** /en → Nähe | distance |
| *in einer Entfernung von* | *at a distance of* |
| *aus der Entfernung* | *from a distance* |
| **ent'gegengesetzt** | opposed, contrary |
| *in der entgegengesetzten Richtung* | *in the opposite direction* |
| **ent'halten** ie-a/ä | to contain, to hold |
| **ent'scheiden** ie-ie **(über)** | to decide (on) |
| *entschieden* | *certainly* |
| *die Entscheidung* | *decision* |
| *eine Entscheidung treffen* | *to come to a decision* |
| **sich ent'schließen** o-o | to decide, to make up o's mind |
| *ich habe mich entschlossen* | *I have made up my mind* |
| **ent'schlossen sein** → unentschlossen sein | to be determined/resolved |
| **der Ent'schluß** sses/üsse | decision |
| *einen Entschluß fassen* | *to take a decision* |
| **ent'schuldigen** | to excuse |
| *entschuldigen Sie! Entschuldigung!* | (*I beg your*) *pardon!* (*I am*) *sorry!* |
| **ent'stehen** a-a → vergehen | to arise, to come into being |

| | |
|---|---|
| **enttäuschen** | to disappoint |
| **ent'wickeln** | to develop |
| *einen Film entwickeln* | *to develop a film* |
| **die Ent'wicklung** /en | development |
| **er'blicken** | to catch sight of |
| **die 'Erde** /n | earth; world; ground |
| *auf der ganzen Erde* | *all the world over* |
| *unter der Erde* | *underground* |
| **das Er'eignis** ses/se | event |
| **er'fahren** u-a/ä | to hear, to learn (of), to experience |
| *erfahren (in)* | *well versed (in), at home (in)* |
| **die Er'fahrung** /en | experience |
| *aus Erfahrung* | *from experience* |
| **der Er'finder** s/- | inventor |
| *die Erfindung* | *invention* |
| **der Er'folg** s/e → Mißerfolg | success |
| *Erfolg haben* | *to succeed (in), to meet with success* |
| **das Er'gebnis** ses/se | result, effect |
| **er'greifen** i-i | to seize, to take, to get hold of, to catch |
| *das Wort ergreifen* | *to (begin to) speak* |
| *Partei ergreifen (für)* | *to take sides (with)* |
| *ergriffen sein* | *to be moved* |
| **er'halten** ie-a/ä | to receive, to get; to preserve |
| *einen Brief erhalten* | *to receive a letter* |
| *einen Platz erhalten* | *to get a seat* |
| *gut erhalten* | *in good condition* |
| **sich er'holen** | to recover |
| **er'innern** | to remind (of) |
| **sich er'innern (an)** → vergessen | to remember |
| *ich erinnere mich, daß* | *I remember that* |
| **die Er'innerung** /en | memory |

| | |
|---|---|
| *zur Erinnerung (an)* | *in memory (of)* |
| **sich er'kälten** | to catch (a) cold |
| *die Erkältung* | *cold* |
| **er'kennen** a-a | to recognize; to realize |
| **er'klären** | to explain; to declare |
| **die Er'klärung** /en | explanation; declaration |
| *eine Erklärung abgeben* | *to make a statement* |
| **er'lauben** → verbieten | to permit, to allow |
| **die Er'laubnis** → Verbot | permission |
| *um die Erlaubnis bitten* | *to ask for permission (to)* |
| *der Erlaubnisschein* | *permit* |
| **ernst** → heiter / komisch | serious, earnest; grave |
| *es ernst meinen* | *to be serious* |
| *im Ernst* | *seriously, in earnest* |
| **die 'Ernte** /n | crop; harvest |
| *eine gute Kartoffelernte* | *a good crop of potatoes* |
| *ernten* | *to harvest, to gather* |
| **er'reichen** → verpassen | to reach; to get |
| *den Zug erreichen* | *to catch the train* |
| *jdn telephonisch erreichen* | *to get s.o. on the phone* |
| *das Ziel erreichen* | *to gain o's end* |
| **er'scheinen** ie-ie | to appear, to turn up |
| *soeben erschienen* | *just published* |
| **er'setzen** | to replace |
| *das Ersatzteil* | *spare part* |
| **erst** | first; only |
| *erst . . . dann* | *first . . . then* |
| *erst gestern* | *only yesterday* |
| *erst heute* | *not until today* |
| *erst morgen* | *not until tomorrow* |
| *erst wenn / als* | *not until* |
| *er ist erst 4 (Jahre alt)* | *he is only four (years old)* |
| **er'staunt sein (über)** | to be astonished (at) |
| *erstaunlich* | *astonishing, amazing* |
| *das Erstaunen* | *astonishment* |
| **der / die / das 'erste** | the first |
| *der Erste des Monats* | *the first day of the month* |

| | |
|---|---|
| *der Erste in der Klasse* | *top of the class* |
| *in erster Linie* | *in the first place* |
| *erstklassig* | *first-class* |
| **'erstmal** | first of all |
| **er'wähnen** | to mention |
| **er'warten** | to wait for; to expect (from) |
| *wider Erwarten* | *contrary to expectation* |
| **er'werben** a-o/i | to gain, to acquire |
| **er'zählen** | to tell |
| *eine Geschichte erzählen* | *to tell a story* |
| *die Erzählung* | *tale, story* |
| **er'zeugen** → vernichten | to produce |
| *das Erzeugnis* | *product* |
| *deutsches Erzeugnis* | *made in Germany* |
| *die Erzeugung* | *production* |
| **er'ziehen** o-o | to educate, to bring up |
| *die Erziehung* | *education* |
| **'essen** a-e/i | to eat; to take o's meal |
| *(zu) Mittag essen* | *to have lunch* |
| **das 'Essen** s/- | meal |
| *das Essen kochen* | *to cook the meal* |
| *das Eßzimmer* | *dining-room* |
| **'etwa** | about; perhaps; by any chance |
| *etwa 10 Jahre* | *about 10 years (or so)* |
| *etwa 100* | *about 100* |
| **'etwas** | something; a little/bit |
| *etwas anderes* | *something else* |
| *etwas Geld* | *some money* |
| *noch etwas?* | *(would you like) some more/anything else?* |
| *so etwas* | *something like that* |
| *etwas Gutes* | *something good* |
| *es geht mir etwas besser* | *I feel a bit better* |

## F

| | |
|---|---|
| **die Fa'brik** /en | factory, mill, works |
| **das Fach** s/ä-er | compartment; field |
| **der 'Faden** s/ä | thread |
| *den Faden verlieren* | *to lose the thread* |
| *der Bindfaden* | *string* |
| *mit Bindfaden zubinden* | *to tie up with string* |
| *einfädeln* | *to thread* |
| **'fähig (zu)** → unfähig | capable (of), able (to) |
| *zu allem fähig* | *capable of anything* |
| *die Fähigkeit* | *(cap)ability* |
| **die 'Fahne** /n | flag |
| **'fahren** u-a/ä | to go; to drive |
| *rechts fahren* | *to drive on the right* |
| *Rechts fahren!* | *Keep to the right* |
| *mit dem Auto fahren* | *to travel by car* |
| *mit der Bahn fahren* | *to go by train/rail* |
| *mit dem Rad fahren* | *to go by bike* |
| *mit dem Zug fahren* | *to take the train* |
| *Langsam fahren!* | *Drive slowly* |
| **der 'Fahrer** s/- | driver |
| **die 'Fahrkarte** /n | ticket |
| *eine Fahrkarte lösen* | *to take a ticket* |
| *Rückfahrkarte* | *return (ticket)* |
| *der Fahrschein* | *ticket* |
| *noch jemand ohne Fahrschein?* | *(any more) fares, please?* |
| **das 'Fahrrad** s/ä-er | bicycle |
| **die 'Fahrschule** /n | driving school |
| **die Fahrt** /en | drive, ride, journey, trip |
| *gute Fahrt!* | *bon voyage!* |
| *in Fahrt sein* | *to be in full swing* |
| **der Fall** s/ä-e | case |
| *auf jeden Fall* | *in any case, at any rate* |
| *auf keinen Fall* | *by no means* |
| **der Fall** s/ä-e | fall |

| | |
|---|---|
| *zu Fall bringen* | *to bring down* |
| **'fallen** ie-a/ä → steigen | to fall, to drop |
| *fallen lassen* | *to drop* |
| *es fällt mir ein* | *it occurs to me* |
| *es fällt mir schwer* | *it's difficult for me* |
| **falsch** → richtig / echt | false, wrong |
| *falsch verstehen* | *to misunderstand* |
| *falsch singen* | *to sing out of tune* |
| *falsch verbunden!* | *sorry, wrong number!* |
| *es ist etwas falsch* | *there is something wrong* |
| *die Uhr geht falsch* | *the watch/clock is wrong* |
| *auf der falschen Seite* | *on the wrong side* |
| **'falten** | to fold |
| *einmal falten* | *to fold in two* |
| *doppelt falten* | *to fold in four* |
| **die Fa'milie** /n | family |
| *Familie haben* | *to have children* |
| *im Kreise der Familie* | *within the family* |
| *der Familienname* | *family name, surname* |
| **fand** (1st, 3rd pers sg pret of **finden**) | |
| **'fangen** i-a/ä | to catch |
| *den Ball fangen* | *to catch the ball* |
| *Feuer fangen* | *to catch fire* |
| **die 'Farbe** /n | colour; paint |
| *was für eine Farbe hat es?* | *what colour is it?* |
| *der Farbfilm* | *colour film* |
| *der Farbstift* | *coloured pencil* |
| *farbig* | *coloured* |
| **'fassen** | to seize, to catch; to hold |
| *an der Hand fassen* | *to take by the hand* |
| *der Saal faßt 1000 Personen* | *the hall holds 1000 people* |
| *sich ein Herz fassen* | *to take courage* |
| *Fasse dich kurz!* | *Make it short!* |
| **fast** / beinahe | almost, nearly |
| **faul** → fleißig | lazy, idle |

| | |
|---|---|
| **die Faust** /äu-e | fist |
| *ein Faustschlag* | *a blow with the fist* |
| *die Faust ballen* | *to clench o's fist* |
| **die 'Feder** /n | feather; pen |
| *der Federhalter* | *penholder* |
| **'fegen** / kehren | to sweep |
| **'fehlen** → da sein | to be absent/missing |
| *was fehlt Ihnen?* | *what is wrong with you?* |
| **der 'Fehler** s/- | mistake; fault, defect |
| *ein leichter / schwerer Fehler* | *a slight/bad mistake* |
| *einen Fehler machen* | *to make a mistake* |
| *einen Fehler haben* | *to have (got) a fault* |
| **'feiern** | to celebrate; to be off work |
| **fein** → unfein / grob | fine, choice, great |
| *es schmeckt fein* | *it tastes delicious* |
| *ein feiner Mensch* | *a refined man* |
| **der Feind** es/e → Freund | enemy |
| *feindlich* | *hostile* |
| **das Feld** s/er | field |
| *das Feld bestellen* | *to till the ground* |
| *auf freiem Feld* | *in the open country* |
| **das Fell** s/e | skin, fur |
| *ein dickes Fell haben* | *to have a thick skin* |
| **der Fels** en/en | rock |
| **das 'Fenster** s/- | window |
| *aus dem Fenster sehen* | *to look out of the window* |
| *die Fensterscheibe* | *window pane* |
| **die 'Ferien** pl | holidays |
| *Ferien machen* | *to take o's holidays* |
| *Ferien haben* | *to be on holiday* |
| *in die Ferien gehen* | *to go on holiday* |
| *die Ferien verbringen* | *to spend o's holidays* |
| *der Ferienkurs* | *vacation course* |
| *das Ferienlager* | *holiday camp* |

| | |
|---|---|
| *die Ferienreise* | *holiday trip* |
| **fern** → nahe | far, distant |
| *von fern* | *from a distance* |
| *fern der Heimat* | *far from home* |
| **die 'Ferne** /n → Nähe | distance |
| *in der Ferne* | *in the distance* |
| *aus der Ferne* | *from a distance* |
| **'ferner** | further(more), moreover |
| **das 'Ferngespräch** s/e → Ortsgespräch | trunk call |
| *fernmündlich* | *by telephone* |
| *der Fernruf* | *telephone call* |
| **das 'Fernsehen** | television |
| *fernsehen* | *to watch television* |
| *im Fernsehen* | *on television* |
| *der Fernsehapparat* | *television set* |
| *der Fernsehzuschauer* | *(tele)viewer* |
| **der 'Fernsprecher** s/- (s. Telefon) | telephone |
| *öffentlicher Fernsprecher* | *public telephone* |
| *das Fernsprechbuch* | *telephone directory, phone-book* |
| *im Fernsprechbuch nachsehen* | *to look up in the phone-book* |
| *die Fernsprechnummer* | *telephone number* |
| *die Fernsprechzelle* | *telephone box* |
| **'fertig** | ready; finished |
| *fertig sein* | *to have finished* |
| *sich fertig machen* | *to get ready* |
| *fertig! los!* | *ready? go!* |
| **das Fest** es/e | feast |
| *ein frohes Fest* | *a pleasant holiday* |
| *der Festtag* | *holiday* |
| **fest** | firm; solid; fixed |
| *festes Land* | *dry land* |
| *fest schlafen* | *to be fast asleep* |
| *zu festen Preisen* | *at fixed prices* |

| | |
|---|---|
| **'fest\|halten** ie-a/ä → los-lassen | to hold, keep |
| *sich festhalten (an)* | *to hold on (to)* |
| *Bitte festhalten!* | *Hold tight there!* |
| **'fest\|machen** → los-machen | to attach/fasten (to); to fix |
| **'fest\|stellen** | to ascertain, to state |
| **fett** → mager | fat |
| *das Fett* | *grease* |
| *der Fettfleck* | *grease mark* |
| **feucht** → trocken | damp |
| **das 'Feuer** s/- | fire |
| *Feuer!* | *Fire!* |
| *Feuer (an)machen* | *to light a fire* |
| *haben Sie Feuer?* | *have you got a light?* |
| *Achtung, Feuergefahr!* | *Danger of fire* |
| *der Feuerlöscher* | *fire extinguisher* |
| **das 'Fieber** s/- | fever |
| *Fieber haben, fiebern* | *to have a temperature* |
| **fiel** (1st, 3rd pers sg pret of **fallen**) | |
| **der Film** s/e | film, picture |
| *einen Film drehen* | *to shoot a film* |
| **'finden** a-u → verlieren | to find |
| **der 'Finger** s/- | finger |
| *sich in den Finger schnei-den* | *to cut o's finger* |
| *sich die Finger verbrennen* | *to burn o's fingers* |
| **'finster** → hell / heiter | dark |
| *es wird finster* | *it is getting dark* |
| *die Finsternis* | *darkness* |
| **die 'Firma** /Firmen | firm, house |
| **der Fisch** s/e | fish |
| *Fische fangen* | *to fish* |
| *fischen* | *to fish* |
| *der Fischer* | *fisherman* |
| **flach** | flat, plain |
| *mit der flachen Hand* | *with the flat of o's hand* |

| | |
|---|---|
| *das flache Land* | *flat country, plain* |
| **die 'Flamme** /n | flame |
| *in Flammen* | *in flames* |
| **die 'Flasche** /n | bottle |
| *eine Flasche Wein* | *a bottle of wine* |
| *eine Weinflasche* | *a wine bottle* |
| **das Fleisch** es | meat; flesh |
| *die Fleischbrühe* | *beef-tea* |
| *der Fleischer* | *butcher* |
| **der Fleiß** es | application, industry |
| *durch Fleiß* | *by hard work* |
| *fleißig* | *hard-working, industrious* |
| *fleißig arbeiten* | *to work hard, to be a hard worker* |
| **'flicken** | to mend/repair |
| **die 'Fliege** /n | fly |
| **'fliegen** o-o | to fly; to travel by air |
| **'fliehen** o-o | to flee/fly; to escape |
| **'fließen** o-o | to flow, to run |
| *fließen (in)* | *to flow (into)* |
| *mit fließendem Wasser* | *with running water* |
| *fließend sprechen* | *to speak fluently* |
| **die Flucht** | flight |
| *die Flucht ergreifen* | *to take to flight, to flee/fly* |
| *flüchten* | *to take refuge* |
| **der 'Flüchtling** s/e | refugee |
| **der Flug** s/ü-e | flight |
| *der Flugplatz* | *airport* |
| **der 'Flügel** s/- | wing; grand piano |
| **das 'Flugzeug** s/e | aeroplane |
| *mit dem Flugzeug* | *by plane* |
| **der Fluß** sses/üsse | river |
| **'flüssig** → fest | liquid |
| *die Flüssigkeit* | *liquid* |
| **die 'Folge** /n | sequel; consequence |
| *zur Folge haben* | *to result in* |
| **'folgen** → vorausgehen | to follow |

| | |
|---|---|
| *einem Beispiel folgen* | *to follow an example* |
| *wie folgt* | *as follows* |
| *am folgenden Tage* | *the following/next day* |
| *folglich* | *consequently, therefore* |
| **'fordern** → gewähren | to demand, to claim, to ask |
| **die Form** /en | form, shape |
| *in Form sein* | *to be in good form* |
| *formen* | *to shape* |
| **der 'Forscher** s/- | researcher, scientist |
| *forschen (nach)* | *to search (for)* |
| *die Forschung* | *research (work)* |
| **fort** → da | gone; away, off |
| *in einem fort* | *on and on* |
| *und so fort* | *and so on* |
| *ich muß fort* | *I must be off* |
| *fort!* | *go away!* |
| **'fort\|fahren** u-a/ä → anhalten / aufhören | to continue, to keep on, to go on |
| **der 'Fortschritt** es/e | progress |
| *Fortschritte machen* | *to make progress, to progress* |
| **'fort\|setzen** → beenden | to continue, to pursue |
| **die 'Fortsetzung** /en | sequel |
| *Fortsetzung folgt* | *To be continued* |
| **das 'Foto** s/s | photo, picture |
| *der Fotoapparat* | *camera* |
| **fotogra'fieren** | to photograph, to take a picture (of) |
| **die 'Frage** /n → Antwort | question |
| *eine Frage stellen* | *to ask a question* |
| *eine Frage aufwerfen* | *to raise a question* |
| *eine Frage beantworten* | *to answer a question* |
| *das ist eine andere Frage* | *that's another question* |
| *das kommt nicht in Frage* | *that's out of the question* |
| **'fragen** → antworten | to ask |
| *ich frage mich, warum* | *I wonder why* |
| *das frage ich dich* | *I'm asking you* |

| | |
|---|---|
| **'Frankreich** s | France |
| **der Fran'zose** n/n | Frenchman |
| *er ist Franzose* | *he is French* |
| **fran'zösisch** | French |
| *auf französisch* | *in French* |
| *er kann Französisch* | *he speaks French* |
| *die französische Sprache* | *the French language* |
| **die Frau** /en | woman; wife |
| *Frau X* | *Mrs X* |
| *gnädige Frau!* | *Madam!* |
| **das 'Fräulein** s/- | young lady |
| *Fräulein X* | *Miss X* |
| **frei** → unfrei / besetzt | free; vacant |
| *Eintritt frei!* | *Admission free* |
| *wir haben frei* | *we have a holiday* |
| *ist der Platz frei?* | *is this seat vacant?* |
| *im Freien* | *in the open (air)* |
| *eine Zeile frei lassen* | *to leave a line blank* |
| **die 'Freiheit** /en | liberty; freedom |
| *in Freiheit* | *in freedom* |
| **'freilich** | yes, indeed; sure enough |
| **die 'Freizeit** | leisure, spare time |
| **fremd** | strange; foreign |
| *ich bin hier fremd* | *I am a stranger here* |
| *fremde Sprachen* | *foreign languages* |
| **der 'Fremde** n/n | stranger; foreigner |
| **'fressen** a-e/i | to eat, to devour |
| **die 'Freude** /n → Leid | joy, pleasure |
| *seine Freude haben (an)* | *to take pleasure (in)* |
| *jdm eine Freude machen* | *to give pleasure to s.o.* |
| *mit Freuden* | *with pleasure* |
| *freudestrahlend* | *beaming with joy* |
| **'freudig** → traurig | joyful |
| *ein freudiges Ereignis* | *a happy event* |
| **sich 'freuen** → leiden | to be pleased (with) |
| *es freut mich* | *I am happy/glad* |
| *sich auf etwas freuen* | *to look forward to sth.* |

| | |
|---|---|
| **der Freund** es/e → Feind / Gegner | friend |
| *ein Freund von mir* | *a friend of mine* |
| *die Freundschaft* | *friendship* |
| *aus Freundschaft* | *out of friendship* |
| *Freundschaft schließen (mit)* | *to make friends* (*with*) |
| **'freundlich** | friendly, kind(ly) |
| *freundliche Grüße* | *kind regards* |
| *das ist sehr freundlich von Ihnen* | *that is very kind of you* |
| *seien Sie so freundlich* | *be kind enough* (*to*) |
| **der 'Frieden** s → Krieg | peace |
| *laß mich in Frieden!* | *leave me alone!* |
| *friedlich* | *peaceable; peaceful* |
| **'frieren** o-o | to freeze; to be cold |
| *ich friere / mich friert* | *I am cold* |
| *es friert* | *it is freezing* |
| **frisch** | fresh |
| *frisch halten* | *to keep fresh* |
| *Frisch gestrichen!* | *Wet paint* |
| *es ist frisch* | *it is cool* |
| **froh** → traurig | glad, joyful, gay |
| *eine frohe Nachricht* | *good news* |
| **'fröhlich** → traurig | merry, cheerful |
| *Fröhliche Weihnachten!* | *Merry Christmas!* |
| **die Frucht** /ü-e | fruit |
| **früh** → spät | early, in good time |
| *am frühen Morgen* | *early in the morning* |
| *heute früh* | *this morning* |
| *morgen früh* | *tomorrow morning* |
| *von früh bis spät* | *from morning till night* |
| *zu früh kommen* | *to be early* |
| *früh aufstehen* | *to get up early* |
| **'früher** → später | sooner; in the past |
| *früher oder später* | *sooner or later* |
| **das 'Frühjahr** s/ **der 'Frühling** s/e | spring |

| | |
|---|---|
| *im Frühling* | *in spring* |
| **das 'Frühstück** s | breakfast |
| *zum Frühstück* | *for breakfast* |
| *frühstücken* | *to have breakfast* |
| **'fühlen** | to feel |
| *sich wohl fühlen* | *to feel well* |
| **fuhr** (1st, 3rd pers sg pret of **fahren**) | |
| **'führen** | to lead, to drive; to take; to direct |
| *das führt zu nichts* | *that leads us nowhere* |
| *an der Leine führen* | *to keep on the lead* |
| *ein Gespräch führen* | *to have a talk* |
| **der 'Führerschein** s/e | driving licence |
| **'füllen (mit)** | to fill (with) |
| *der Füller* | *fountain pen* |
| **der Funk** s | wireless, radio, sound |
| *im Funk* | *on the wireless/radio* |
| **die Furcht** | fear |
| *aus Furcht (vor)* | *for fear* (*of*) |
| *Furcht haben (vor)* | *to be afraid* (*of*) |
| **'furchtbar** | terrible, awful |
| **'fürchten, sich fürchten (vor)** | to be afraid of; to fear |
| *fürchterlich* | *dreadful* |
| **der Fuß** es/ü-e | foot |
| *zu Fuß* | *on foot* |
| *zu Fuß gehen* | *to walk* |
| *gut zu Fuß sein* | *to be a good walker* |
| *auf gutem Fuß stehen (mit)* | *to be on good terms* (*with*) |
| *der Fußboden* | *floor* |
| *der Fußgänger* | *pedestrian* |
| **der 'Fußball** s/ä-e | football |
| *Fußball spielen* | *to play football* |
| **'füttern** | to feed |

## G

| | |
|---|---|
| **gab** (1st, 3rd pers sg pret of **geben**) | gave |
| **die 'Gabe** /n; / Geschenk | gift; present |
| **die 'Gabel** /n | fork |
| *mit der Gabel essen* | *to eat with a fork* |
| **der Gang** s/ä-e | walk(ing); way; speed/ gear |
| *in Gang bringen* | *to get going, to start up* |
| *in Gang sein* | *to be on, to be in full swing* |
| *in Gang halten* | *to keep going* |
| *im dritten Gang* | *in third (gear)* |
| *sich in Gang setzen* | *to start; to begin to move* |
| **ganz** | quite, whole; wholly, entirely |
| *von ganzem Herzen* | *with all (my) heart* |
| *ganz in der Nähe* | *close by* |
| *ganz gut* | *quite good, not bad* |
| *ganz gewiß* | *most certainly* |
| *ganz und gar* | *wholly, altogether* |
| *ganz und gar nicht* | *not at all, by no means* |
| **gar nicht** | not at all |
| **gar nichts** | nothing at all |
| **die Gar'dine** /n | curtain |
| **der 'Garten** s/ä | garden |
| **das Gas** es/e | gas |
| *Gas geben* | *to step on the accelerator* |
| **der Gast** es/ä-e | guest |
| *Gäste haben* | *to have company* |
| **das 'Gasthaus** es/äu-er | hotel, restaurant |
| *die Gaststätte* | *restaurant* |
| **das Ge'bäude** s/- | building |
| *das öffentliche Gebäude* | *public building* |
| **'geben** a-e/i | to give |
| *es gibt* | *there is/are* |
| *was gibt's?* | *what is the matter?* |

| | |
|---|---|
| *was gibt's Neues?* | *what's the news?* |
| das **Ge'biet** s/e | field; district |
| *auf diesem Gebiet* | *in this field* |
| **ge'bildet** (past part of bilden) | educated, cultured |
| das **Ge'birge** s/- | mountains *pl* |
| *im Gebirge* | *in the mountains* |
| **ge'blieben** (past part of bleiben) | |
| **ge'boren** → gestorben | born |
| *wann sind Sie geboren?* | *when were you born?* |
| *wo sind Sie geboren?* | *where were you born?* |
| *geboren werden* | *to be born* |
| *ich bin 1945 geboren* | *I was born in 1945* |
| *Goethe wurde 1749 geboren* | *Goethe was born in 1749* |
| *Frau X geb(orene) Y* | *Mrs X* née *Y* |
| **ge'bracht** (past part of bringen) | |
| der **Ge'brauch** s/ä-e | use |
| *Gebrauch machen (von)* | *to make use (of)* |
| *in Gebrauch* | *in use* |
| *außer Gebrauch* | *out of use* |
| **ge'brauchen** | to use, to make use of |
| *gebraucht* | *used, second-hand* |
| *der Gebrauchtwagen* | *used car* |
| *zu nichts zu gebrauchen* | *no use* |
| die **Ge'burt** /en → Tod | birth |
| *von Geburt Deutscher* | *German-born* |
| *Geburtsort und -tag* | *place and date of birth* |
| der **Ge'burtstag** s/e | birthday |
| **ge'dacht** (past part of denken) | |
| das **Ge'dächtnis** ses se | memory |
| *aus dem Gedächtnis* | *by heart, from memory* |
| *zum Gedächtnis (an)* | *in memory (of)* |
| *im Gedächtnis behalten* | *to bear in mind* |
| der **Ge'danke** ns/n | thought, idea |

| | |
|---|---|
| *der bloße Gedanke* | *the very thought* (*of it*) |
| *kein Gedanke!* | *nothing of the kind!* |
| *sich Gedanken machen (über)* | *to worry* (*about*) |
| **das Ge'dicht** es/e | poem |
| **die Ge'duld** | patience |
| *Geduld haben* | *to have patience* |
| *die Geduld verlieren* | *to lose patience* |
| (Sehr) **ge'ehrter** Herr! | (Dear) Sir, |
| **die Ge'fahr** /en | danger |
| *in Gefahr* | *in danger* |
| *außer Gefahr* | *out of danger* |
| *Gefahr laufen (zu)* | *to run the risk* (*of*) |
| **ge'fährlich** | dangerous |
| **der Ge'fährte** n/n | companion, fellow |
| **ge'fallen** ie-a/ä | to please |
| *wie gefällt Ihnen . . .?* | *how do you like . . .?* |
| *es gefällt mir (sehr)* | *I like it* (*very much*) |
| *gefällt Ihnen das?* | *do you like it?* |
| *Gefallen finden (an)* | *to enjoy* |
| *einen Gefallen tun* | *to do a favour* |
| *tun Sie mir den Gefallen* | *be so kind* (*as to*); *do me the favour* |
| **das Ge'fängnis** ses/se | prison |
| **das Ge'fühl** s/e | feeling |
| **ge'funden** (past part of **finden**) | |
| **ge'gangen** (past part of **gehen**) | |
| **die 'Gegend** /en | region; country; quarter |
| *in der Gegend von* | *near, close to* |
| **'gegeneinander** | towards, against each other/one another |
| **der 'Gegenstand** s/ä-e | object; subject |
| **das 'Gegenteil** s | contrary, opposite |
| *im Gegenteil* | *on the contrary* |
| **gegen'über** | opposite |
| *gerade gegenüber* | *immediately opposite* |

| | |
|---|---|
| *mir gegenüber* | *facing/opposite me* |
| **die 'Gegenwart** | presence |
| *in Gegenwart von* | *in the presence of* |
| **'gegenwärtig** | at present |
| **der 'Gegner s/-** → Freund | adversary, enemy |
| **Geh!** → Halt | Go |
| **das Ge'halt s/ä-er** | salary; pay |
| *das Monatsgehalt* | *monthly salary/pay* |
| **ge'heim** | secret |
| *das Geheimnis* | *secret* |
| *geheimnisvoll* | *mysterious* |
| **'gehen i-a** | to go, to walk |
| *wie geht es Ihnen?* | *how are you?* |
| *es geht mir gut* | *I am well; I am doing well* |
| *es geht mir besser* | *I am better; I feel better* |
| *wie geht's?* | *how are you?* |
| *es wird schon gehen* | *it will be all right* |
| *es geht (dar)um* | *it's a matter/question (of)* |
| *das geht nicht* | *it can't be done* |
| *das geht Sie nichts an* | *that's none of your business* |
| *laß mich gehen!* | *leave me alone* |
| **ge'horchen** | to obey |
| **ge'hören (zu)** | to belong (to); to form part of |
| *das gehört mir* | *that's mine* |
| *es gehört sich* | *it's proper* |
| *das gehört sich nicht* | *it's not done* |
| **der Geist es/er** | mind, spirit |
| *die Geistesgegenwart* | *presence of mind* |
| *geistig* | *intellectual, mental; spiritual* |
| **gelb** | yellow |
| **das Geld es/er** | money; change |
| *Geld verdienen* | *to make money* |

| | |
|---|---|
| *Geld verlieren* | *to lose money* |
| *ich habe kein Geld bei mir* | *I've no money on me* |
| *das kostet viel Geld* | *that costs a lot (of money)* |
| *das Geldstück* | *coin* |
| **die Ge'legenheit** /en | occasion; chance |
| *bei Gelegenheit* | *on occasion* |
| *bei dieser Gelegenheit* | *on that occasion* |
| *die Gelegenheit ergreifen/verpassen* | *to seize/miss the opportunity* |
| *gelegentlich* | *sometime or other* |
| **ge'lehrt** | learned |
| **ge'lingen** a-u → mißlingen | to succeed |
| *es ist mir gelungen (zu)* | *I have succeeded (in)* |
| **'gelten** a-o/i | to count (for) |
| *das gilt nicht* | *that doesn't count* |
| **ge'mein** | common; vulgar, base |
| **das Ge'müse** s/ Gemüsesorten | vegetable(s) |
| **ge'mütlich** → ungemütlich | sociable, comfortable |
| *hier ist es gemütlich* | *here you feel at home* |
| *die gemütliche Ecke* | *cosy corner* |
| *in aller Gemütlichkeit* | *in a leisurely fashion* |
| **ge'nau** → ungefähr | just, exact, exactly |
| *die genaue Zeit* | *the right time* |
| *die Uhr geht genau* | *this watch/clock keeps good time* |
| *es ist genau 3 Uhr* | *it's 3 o'clock sharp* |
| *genau ein Pfund* | *exactly one pound* |
| *genaugenommen* | *strictly speaking* |
| **ge'nießen** o-o | to enjoy |
| **ge'nommen** (past part of **nehmen**) | |
| **der Ge'nosse** n/n | comrade |
| *der Zeitgenosse* | *contemporary* |
| **ge'nug** | enough |

| | |
|---|---|
| *Geld genug* | *enough money* |
| *genug!* | *enough! that will do!* |
| **ge'nügen** | to be enough |
| *das genügt* | *that will do* |
| **ge'öffnet** (past part of öffnen) → geschlossen | open |
| **das Ge'päck** s | luggage, baggage |
| *das Gepäck aufgeben* | *to register o's luggage* |
| *der Gepäckträger* | *porter; carrier* |
| **ge'rade** → krumm | straight |
| *eine gerade Linie* | *a straight line* |
| *geradeaus* | *straight ahead* |
| *gehen Sie geradeaus* | *keep straight on* |
| **ge'rade** *adv* | just, directly, precisely, just now |
| *es ist gerade 10 Uhr* | *it's just 10 (o'clock)* |
| *er ist gerade fort* | *he has just left* |
| *ich wollte gerade weggehen* | *I was just about to leave* |
| *gerade gegenüber* | *just opposite* |
| **das Ge'rät** es/e | tool; apparatus, set |
| *dieses Gerät dient zum . . .* | *this gadget is used for . . .* |
| **das Ge'räusch** es/e | noise |
| *ein leises Geräusch* | *a slight noise* |
| *beim leisesten Geräusch* | *at the slightest noise* |
| **ge'recht** → ungerecht | just |
| *eine gerechte Sache* | *a just cause* |
| *eine gerechte Strafe* | *a well-deserved punishment* |
| *die Gerechtigkeit* | *justice* |
| **das Ge'richt** s/e | court; dish |
| **ge'ring** | little, small; low; of inferior quality |
| *nicht im geringsten* | *not in the (very) least* |
| *nicht die geringste Ahnung* | *not the faintest idea* |
| **gern** / lieber / am liebsten | gladly, with pleasure |
| *herzlich gern* | *with great pleasure* |

| | |
|---|---|
| *gern geschehen!* | *don't mention it* |
| *gern haben* | *to be fond of, to like/love* |
| *ich möchte gern* | *I'd like to* |
| *ich möchte gern wissen* | *I wonder* |
| *etwas gern tun* | *to like doing s.th.* |
| **der Ge'ruch** s/ü-e | smell |
| *ein angenehmer Geruch* | *a pleasant smell* |
| *ein übler Geruch* | *a bad smell* |
| **der Ge'sang** s/ä-e | song |
| **das Ge'schäft** s/e | shop; business |
| *Geschäfte machen* | *to do business* |
| *ein gutes Geschäft* | *a good bargain* |
| *ein Geschäftsmann* | *a businessman* |
| *die Geschäftszeit* | *hours of business* |
| **ge'schehen** a-e/ie | to happen, to come about |
| *was ist geschehen?* | *what has happened?* |
| *gern geschehen!* | *don't mention it* |
| *geschieht ihm recht!* | *serves him right!* |
| *es ist ein Unglück geschehen* | *there has been an accident* |
| **das Ge'schenk** s/e | gift, present |
| **die Ge'schichte** | history; story |
| *die Geschichte Deutschlands* | *the history of Germany* |
| *eine Geschichte erzählen* | *to tell a story* |
| *eine schöne Geschichte!* | *a pretty mess!* |
| **ge'schickt** | clever, skilful |
| **ge'schlossen** (past part of **schließen**) → geöffnet | shut |
| **der Ge'schmack** s/ä-e | taste |
| *das ist nicht nach meinem Geschmack* | *that's not to my taste* |
| *geschmackvoll* | *in good taste* |
| **ge'schrieben** (past part of **schreiben**) | written |
| **die Ge'schwindigkeit** /en | speed |

| | |
|---|---|
| *mit Höchstgeschwindigkeit* | *at top speed* |
| *mit einer Geschwindigkeit von ...* | *at a speed of ...* |
| **die Ge'sellschaft** /en | society; company |
| *in guter Gesellschaft* | *in good company* |
| *eine Gesellschaft geben* | *to give a party* |
| *jdm Gesellschaft leisten* | *to keep s.o. company* |
| **das Ge'setz** es/e | law |
| **das Ge'sicht** s/er | face |
| *zu Gesicht bekommen* | *to catch sight of* |
| *ins Gesicht sehen* | *to look in the face* |
| *das Gesicht verziehen* | *to make a face* |
| **das Ge'spräch** s/e | conversation, talk |
| *ein Gespräch beginnen* | *to enter into a conversation* |
| *ein Gespräch führen (mit)* | *to have a talk (with)* |
| *das Ortsgespräch* | *local call* |
| *das Ferngespräch* | *trunk call* |
| **ge'sprochen** (past part of **sprechen**) | spoken |
| **die Ge'stalt** /en | form, shape; figure |
| *in Gestalt von* | *in the shape of* |
| *Gestalt annehmen* | *to take shape* |
| *gestalten* | *to form, to shape* |
| **ge'stehen** a-a | to admit, to confess |
| *offen gestanden* | *to be frank* |
| **'gestern** | yesterday |
| *vorgestern* | *the day before yesterday* |
| *gestern früh* | *yesterday morning* |
| *gestern abend* | *last night* |
| **ge'storben** (past part of **sterben**) | died, dead |
| **ge'sund** → krank | healthy, in good health, well, sound |
| *gesund sein* | *to be in good health* |
| *gesund werden* | *to recover* |
| *wieder gesund* | *recovered* |
| *die gesunde Nahrung* | *wholesome food* |

| | |
|---|---|
| *der gesunde Menschenverstand* | *common sense* |
| *die Gesundheit* | *health* |
| **ge'tan** (past part of **tun**) | done |
| **das Ge'tränk** s/e | drink |
| **das Ge'treide** s/ Getreidearten | cereals *pl*, corn/grain |
| **ge'währen** → fordern | to grant |
| **die Ge'walt** /en | power, force |
| *mit Gewalt* | *by force* |
| *gewaltig* | *powerful* |
| **ge'wandt** | skilful |
| *die Gewandtheit* | *skill* |
| **das Ge'wehr** s/e | rifle |
| *das Gewehr laden* | *to load the rifle* |
| *mit dem Gewehr schießen* | *to shoot* |
| **ge'wesen** (past part of **sein**) | been |
| **das Ge'wicht** s/e | weight |
| *ins Gewicht fallen* | *to be of importance* |
| **der Ge'winn** s/e | gain, profit |
| *mit Gewinn verkaufen* | *to sell at a profit* |
| **ge'winnen** a-o | to gain, to win |
| *Zeit gewinnen* | *to gain time* |
| *5:2 (fünf zu zwei) gewinnen* | *to win by 5 goals to 2* |
| *den Lauf gewinnen* | *to win the race* |
| *Kohle gewinnen* | *to mine coal* |
| **ge'wiß** → ungewiß | certain; sure; certainly, surely |
| *gewisse Leute* | *certain people* |
| *ich bin meiner Sache gewiß* | *I am quite certain* |
| *aber gewiß!* | *why certainly!* |
| *ganz gewiß* | *sure enough, no doubt* |
| *gewissermaßen* | *so to speak, as it were* |
| **das Ge'wissen** s | conscience |
| *ein reines Gewissen haben* | *to have a clear conscience* |
| *die Gewissensfreiheit* | *freedom of conscience* |

|  |  |
|---|---|
| **sich ge'wöhnen (an)** | to get accustomed (to)/ used (to) |
| *gewöhnt sein (zu)* | *to be used (to)* |
| **die Ge'wohnheit** /en | habit, custom |
| *aus Gewohnheit* | *from habit* |
| *die Gewohnheit haben (zu)* | *to be in the habit (of)* |
| **ge'wöhnlich** → außergewöhnlich | general, usual |
| *wie gewöhnlich* | *as usual* |
| **ge'worden** (past part of werden) | |
| **gib, gibt** (imp, 3rd pers sg pres of geben) | |
| *es gibt* | *there is/are* |
| **'gießen** o-o | to pour; to water |
| *in ein Glas gießen* | *to pour into a glass* |
| *die Blumen gießen* | *to water the flowers* |
| *es gießt (in Strömen)* | *it's pouring (with rain)* |
| *vollgießen* | *to fill (up)* |
| **das Gift** s/e | poison |
| **ging** (1st, 3rd pers sg pret of gehen) | went |
| **der 'Gipfel** s/- | summit, top |
| *das ist der Gipfel!* | *that's the limit!* |
| **'glänzen** | to shine |
| *glänzend* | *brilliant* |
| **das Glas** es/ä-er | glass |
| *Vorsicht, Glas!* | *Glass, with care* |
| *aus Glas* | *made of glass* |
| *ein Glas Wein* | *a glass of wine* |
| *ein Weinglas* | *a wine glass* |
| *aus einem Glas trinken* | *to drink out of a glass* |
| **glatt** → rauh | smooth; polished; slippery |
| *es ist glatt gegangen* | *it went without a hitch* |
| *glatt machen* | *to smooth; to polish* |

| | |
|---|---|
| **der 'Glaube** ns → Zweifel | faith, belief |
| **'glauben** | to believe; to think |
| *ich glaube es* | *I believe so* |
| *ich glaube ihm* | *I believe him* |
| *ich glaube es ihm* | *I believe what he says* |
| *ich glaube kein Wort davon* | *I don't believe a word of it* |
| **gleich** | like, same; equal; similar |
| *das ist mir gleich* | *it's all the same to (me)* |
| *zu gleicher Zeit* | *at the same time* |
| *gleich alt* | *of the same age* |
| *gleich groß* | *of the same size, equally large* |
| *= (ist) gleich* | *equal(s)/are/make* |
| *2 + 3 = 5* *zwei und drei (ist) gleich 5* | *2 and 3 equal(s)/are/ make 5* |
| *5 − 3 = 2* *fünf weniger drei (ist) gleich 2* | *5 minus 3 equals 2* |
| *2 × 2 = 4* *zwei mal zwei (ist) gleich vier* | *2 times 2 are 4* |
| *4 ÷ 2 = 2* *vier durch zwei (ist) gleich zwei* | *4 divided by 2 equals 2* |
| **gleich** | in a moment, directly, at once |
| *gleich!* | *just a minute, please!* |
| *(ich komme) gleich!* | *(I'm) coming!* |
| *ich bin gleich wieder da* | *I'll be back in a minute* |
| *gleich gegenüber* | *just opposite* |
| *wie heißt er doch gleich?* | *what's his name?* |
| **'gleichen** i-i | to equal; to be like, to resemble |
| **'gleichfalls** | also, as well |
| *danke, gleichfalls!* | *thanks, the same to you!* |
| **die 'Gleichheit** → Ungleichheit | equality |

| | |
|---|---|
| **'gleichzeitig** → nacheinander | at the same time |
| **das Glied** s/er | limb; member |
| **die 'Glocke** /n | bell |
| *die Glocke läuten* | *to ring the bell* |
| *die Glocke läutet* | *the bell is ringing* |
| **das Glück** s → Unglück | (good) luck |
| *zum Glück* | *fortunately* |
| *Glück haben* | *to be lucky* |
| *kein Glück haben* | *to be out of luck* |
| *Glück wünschen* | *to wish good luck* |
| *viel Glück!* | *good luck (to you)!* |
| *auf gut Glück* | *at random* |
| *was für ein Glück!* | *what a piece/stroke of good luck* |
| **'glücklich** → unglücklich | lucky; happy |
| *glückliche Reise!* | *bon voyage!* |
| *glücklich machen* | *to make happy* |
| *glücklicherweise* | *fortunately* |
| **das Gold** es | gold |
| *aus Gold, golden* | *made of gold, golden* |
| **der Gott** es/ö-er | God |
| *ach Gott!* | *Heavens!* |
| *Gott sei Dank!* | *thank God! fortunately!* |
| *in Gottes Namen!* | *for Heaven's sake!* |
| **'graben** u-a/ä | to dig |
| *ein Loch graben* | *to dig a hole* |
| *der Graben* | *ditch* |
| **der Grad** es/e | degree |
| *es sind 20 Grad über/unter Null* | *it's 20 degrees above/below zero* |
| *in einem gewissen Grade* | *to a certain degree* |
| **das Gramm** s/- | gram(me) |
| **das Gras** es/ä-er | grass |
| **grau** | grey |
| **'greifen** i-i | to seize, to reach (for) |

| | |
|---|---|
| *in die Tasche greifen* | *to put o's hand into o's pocket* |
| *unter die Arme greifen* | *to give a helping hand (to)* |
| **die 'Grenze** /n | frontier, border; limit |
| *an der Grenze* | *on the frontier* |
| *über die Grenze fahren, die Grenze überschreiten* | *to cross the frontier* |
| *alles hat seine Grenzen* | *there is a limit to everything* |
| **der Griff** s/e | grip; handle |
| *einen guten Griff tun* | *to make a good choice* |
| *Griff ziehen!* | *Pull the handle* |
| **die 'Grippe** /n | flu |
| *die Grippe haben* | *to have got the flu* |
| **grob** → fein | coarse, rough |
| *ein grober Fehler* | *a bad mistake* |
| *grobe Worte* | *strong terms* |
| **groß** / größer / am größten → klein | great; large, big, tall |
| *ganz groß!* | *great!* |
| *gleich groß* | *of the same size* |
| *immer größer* | *greater and greater* |
| *im großen (und) ganzen* | *generally speaking, on the whole* |
| *wie groß ist er?* | *how tall is he?* |
| *er ist groß geworden* | *he has grown* |
| **'großartig** | grand, wonderful |
| *das ist ja großartig!* | *it's simply grand!* |
| *eine großartige Aussicht* | *a splendid view* |
| **die 'Größe** /n | size; height |
| *sie haben die gleiche Größe* | *they are the same size* |
| **die 'Großmutter** /ü | grandmother |
| *der Großvater* | *grandfather* |
| **'größtenteils** | for the most part, mostly |
| **grün** | green |
| **der Grund** es/ü-e | bottom; reason, cause |

| | |
|---|---|
| *der Meeresgrund* | *bottom of the sea* |
| *im Grunde (genommen)* | *strictly speaking* |
| *aus welchem Grund?* | *for what reason?* |
| *aus diesem Grund* | *for this reason* |
| *aus guten Gründen* | *with reason* |
| *ein triftiger Grund* | *a good reason* |
| *gründen* | *to found, to establish* |
| **der 'Grundsatz** es/ä-e | principle |
| *es sich zum Grundsatz machen* | *to make it a rule* |
| **die 'Gruppe** /n | group |
| *in Gruppen* pl | *in groups* pl |
| *in Gruppen einteilen* | *to form into groups* |
| **der Gruß** es/ü-e | greeting |
| *mit bestem Gruß* | *yours sincerely* |
| *herzliche Grüße* pl | *kind regards* |
| *viele Grüße von mir (an)* | *my kindest regards* (*to*) |
| **'grüßen** | to greet |
| *grüßen Sie ihn von mir* | *give him my kind regards* |
| **'gucken** | to look, to peep |
| **der 'Gummi** s/s | rubber |
| *der Radiergummi* | *india-rubber* |
| *aus Gummi* | *made of rubber* |
| **'günstig** → ungünstig | favourable |
| *eine günstige Gelegenheit* | *a favourable opportunity* |
| **gut** / besser / am besten → schlecht / böse | good; well |
| *das ist ganz gut* | *that's not bad* |
| *schon gut!* | *never mind!* |
| *es geht mir gut* | *I am well* |
| *guten Morgen!* | *good morning!* |
| *guten Tag!* | *how do you do?, good morning/afternoon/evening* |
| *guten Abend!* | *good evening* |
| *gute Nacht!* | *good night* |
| *gut riechen* | *to smell good* |

*gut schmecken* — *to taste good*
*auf gut deutsch* — *in plain English*
*mach's gut!* — *good luck!, have a good time!, cheerio!*

**das Gut** es/ü-er — estate; property

## H

**das Haar** es/e — hair
*sich die Haare schneiden lassen* — *to have o's hair cut*
*Haarschneiden, bitte!* — *hair-cut, please*
**'haben** — to have (got)
*ich hab's!* — *I have (got) it!*
*was hast du?* — *what is the matter with you?*
*den wievielten haben wir?* — *what is the date?*
*wir haben Montag, den 26. März* — *it's Monday, (the) 26th (of) March*
*gern haben* — *to be fond of, to like*
*Geduld haben* — *to be patient*
**der 'Hafen** s/ä — port, harbour
*den Hafen erreichen* — *to get to the port*
**der Hahn** s/ä-e — cock; tap
*den Hahn zudrehen* — *to turn the tap off*
**halb** — half; by halves
*eine halbe Stunde* — *half an hour*
*anderthalb Stunden* — *one hour and a half*
*halb 10 (Uhr)* — *half past nine (o'clock)*
*5 vor halb 10* — *twenty-five (minutes) past 9*
*5 nach halb 10* — *twenty-five to 10 (o'clock)*
*ein halbes Jahr* — *half a year, six months*
*auf halbem Wege* — *half-way*
*eineinhalb / anderthalb* — *one and a half*
**die 'Hälfte** /n — half

| | |
|---|---|
| **die 'Halle** /n | hall |
| **der Hals** es/ä-e | neck; throat |
| *einen schlimmen Hals haben* | *to have a sore throat* |
| **Halt!** → Geh! | Stop! |
| **'halten** ie-a/ä | to hold; to keep; to take; to stop |
| *eine Rede halten* | *to make a speech* |
| *Wort halten* | *to keep o's word* |
| *den Mund halten* | *to keep quiet, shut up* |
| *sich rechts halten* | *keep to the right* |
| *der Zug hält nicht* | *the train does not stop* |
| *halten für* | *to take for, to think* |
| *es für nötig halten* | *to think it necessary* |
| *in der Hand halten* | *to hold in o's hand* |
| *die Haltestelle* | *stop* |
| *Halteverbot!* | *No waiting* |
| **die 'Haltung** /en | attitude |
| **der 'Hammer** s/ä | hammer |
| **die Hand** /ä-e | hand |
| *bei der Hand / zur Hand* | *at hand* |
| *mit der rechten Hand* | *with o's right hand* |
| *zur rechten Hand* | *on the right (hand)* |
| *jdm die Hand drücken / geben* | *to shake hands (with s.o.)* |
| *eine Handvoll* | *a handful (of)* |
| **der 'Handel** s | trade, commerce |
| *Handel treiben (mit)* | *to deal (in)* |
| *handeln* | *to trade; to act* |
| *es handelt sich um* | *it is a question/matter of* |
| *worum handelt es sich?* | *what is the question? what's it about?* |
| **die 'Handlung** /en | action |
| **der 'Handschuh** s/e | glove |
| *die Handschuhe anziehen* | *to put on o's gloves* |
| *ein Paar Handschuhe* | *a pair of gloves* |
| **das 'Handtuch** s/ü-er | towel |
| **das 'Handwerk** s/e | trade |

| | |
|---|---|
| *ein Handwerk lernen* | *to learn a trade* |
| *sein Handwerk verstehen* | *to know o's business* |
| *der Handwerker* | *artisan* |
| **'hängen** i-a | to hang; to be attached (to) |
| *an der Decke hängen* | *to hang from the ceiling* |
| *an den Nagel hängen* | *to give up* |
| *sie hängt an ihrer Mutter* | *she is attached to her mother* |
| **hart** → weich | hard; firm; severe |
| *ein harter Mann* | *a hard man* |
| *harte Worte* pl | *hard words* pl |
| *hart bleiben* | *to stand firm* |
| **'hassen** | to hate |
| **'häßlich** | ugly; mean |
| **hast, hat** (2nd, 3rd pers sg pres of **haben**) | |
| **'häufig** | frequent; frequently, often |
| **das Haupt** es/äu-er | head; chief |
| **die 'Hauptsache** /n | essential; main thing |
| *die Hauptsache ist, daß* | *the (main) point is that* |
| *hauptsächlich* | *main(ly), chiefly)* |
| **die 'Hauptstadt** /ä-e | capital |
| **das Haus** es/äu-er | house |
| *nach Hause gehen* | *to go home* |
| *nach Hause bringen* | *to see home* |
| *zu Hause sein* | *to be at home, to be in* |
| *zu Hause lassen* | *to leave at home* |
| *die Hausfrau* | *housewife* |
| *der Haushalt* | *household* |
| *den Haushalt führen* | *to run the household* |
| **die Haut** /äu-e | skin |
| *helle / dunkle Haut haben* | *to have fair/dark skin* |
| *naß bis auf die Haut* | *soaked to the skin* |
| *er ist nur Haut und Knochen* | *he is nothing but skin and bones* |
| **'heben** o-o | to lift |

| | |
|---|---|
| *die Hand heben* | *to raise o's hand* |
| *sich heben und senken* | *to rise and fall* |
| **das Heer** es/e | army |
| **das Heft** es/e | exercise-book |
| *in ein Heft schreiben* | *to write into an exercise-book* |
| **'heftig** → sanft | violent, hard |
| *heftig werden* | *to get into a temper* |
| *heftig weinen* | *to cry bitterly* |
| **'heilen** | to cure; to heal (up) |
| **'heilig** | holy; sacred |
| *der Heilige Abend* | *Christmas Eve* |
| **das Heim** s/e | home |
| *heim* | *home* |
| **die 'Heimat** → Fremde | home; native country |
| **'heimkehren** / heimkommen | to come (back) home |
| **'heiraten** | to marry; to get married |
| *aus Liebe heiraten* | *to marry for love* |
| *die Heirat* | *marriage* |
| *verheiratet* | *married* |
| **heiß** → kalt | hot |
| *es ist heiß* | *it is hot* |
| *mir ist heiß* | *I feel hot, I am hot* |
| *ist das heiß!* | *how hot it is!* |
| *kochend heiß* | *boiling hot* |
| **'heißen** ie-ei | to be called; to mean |
| *wie heißen Sie?* | *what's your name?* |
| *wie heißt der Ort?* | *what's the name of this place?* |
| *wie heißt das auf deutsch?* | *what is that in German?* |
| *das heißt (d.h.)* | *that is, i.e.* |
| *es heißt* | *they say* |
| *was soll das heißen?* | *what is the meaning of (all) that?* |
| **'heiter** → ernst / finster | clear; gay, cheerful |
| **'heizen** | to heat; to make a fire |
| *die Heizung* | *heating* |

| | |
|---|---|
| **'helfen** a-o/i | to help; to serve |
| *es hilft nichts* | *it's no good* |
| *er weiß sich zu helfen* | *he can look after himself* |
| **hell** → dunkel / finster | clear, bright |
| *es ist hell* | *it is (quite) light* |
| *es wird hell* | *it's beginning to dawn* |
| *hellblau* | *light blue* |
| *seine helle Freude haben (an)* | *to be (more than) delighted at* |
| **das Hemd** s/en | shirt |
| *das Hemd ausziehen* | *to take off o's shirt* |
| *ein frisches Hemd anziehen* | *to put on a clean shirt* |
| **her** → hin | here |
| *komm her!* | *come here* |
| *wie lange ist es her?* | *how long ago is it?* |
| *wo sind Sie her?* | *where do you come from?* |
| *wo haben Sie das her?* | *where did you get that (from)?* |
| **(he)'rauf** → hinunter | up(wards) |
| **(he)'raus** → hinein | out |
| *raus!* | *get out!* |
| *hier heraus* | *this way out* |
| *herausnehmen (aus)* | *to take out (of)* |
| **der Herbst** es/e | autumn |
| *im Herbst* | *in autumn* |
| **der Herd** es/e | stove |
| *der Elektroherd* | *electric cooker* |
| *der Gasherd* | *gas stove* |
| **(he)'rein!** → hinaus! | come in! |
| *hier herein!* | *this way, please!* |
| **he'rein\|kommen** → hinaus\|gehen | to come in(to) |
| **der Herr** n/en | gentleman; master |
| *mein Herr!* | *sir!* |
| *meine Herren!* | *gentlemen!* |
| *(für) Herren* | *Gentlemen('s lavatory* |
| *Herr X* | *Mr X* |
| *(Sehr) geehrter Herr X!* | *Dear Mr. X,* |

| | |
|---|---|
| *Herr Doktor X* | *Doctor X* |
| **'herrlich** | grand, wonderful, glorious |
| **'herrschen** → dienen | to rule |
| *es herrscht Stille* | *silence reigns* |
| **'her\|stellen** | to produce; to turn out |
| *die Herstellung* | *production; output* |
| **he'rum** | about |
| *rings herum* | *round about* |
| *um die Ecke herum* | *round the corner* |
| **(he)'runter** → hinauf | down |
| *herunter!* | *down you go!* |
| *komm herunter!* | *come down!* |
| **her'vorragend** | excellent |
| **das Herz** ens/en | heart |
| *von Herzen gern* | *with the greatest (of) pleasure* |
| *von ganzem Herzen* | *with all my heart* |
| *schweren Herzens* | *with a heavy heart* |
| *es liegt mir am Herzen* | *I have it at heart* |
| **'herzlich** | cordial, affectionate |
| *herzlich gern* | *gladly, with pleasure* |
| *herzliche Grüße* pl | *kind regards* |
| **'heute** | today, this day |
| *heute morgen* | *this morning* |
| *heute vormittag* | *this morning* |
| *heute mittag* | *at noon today* |
| *heute nachmittag* | *this afternoon/evening* |
| *heute abend* | *this evening, tonight* |
| *heute nacht* | *tonight* |
| *noch heute* | *this very day* |
| *bis heute* | *till today, to date* |
| *von heute an* | *from today* |
| *heute in acht Tagen* | *today/this day week* |
| *heute vor acht Tagen* | *a week ago* |
| *welchen (Tag) haben wir heute?* | *what day is it today?* |
| *heute haben wir den 26.* | *today is the 26th* |

| | |
|---|---|
| *heute ist Sonntag, der 26. März* | *today is Sunday, (the) 26th (of) March* |
| **'heutzutage** | nowadays, these days |
| **hielt** (1st, 3rd pers sg pret of **halten**) | |
| **hier** → dort | here |
| *hier und dort* | *here and there* |
| *hier!* | *present! here!* |
| *hier bin ich* | *here I am* |
| **'hierauf** | after this, then |
| **'hierher** → dorthin | here, this way, over here |
| *(komm) hierher!* | *come here* |
| *hier herein, bitte!* | *this way (in), please* |
| **die 'Hilfe /n** | help, relief |
| *Hilfe!* | *help!* |
| *die erste Hilfe* | *first aid* |
| *um Hilfe rufen* | *to call for help* |
| *jdm zu Hilfe eilen* | *to rush to s.o'.s aid* |
| **der 'Himmel s/-** | sky; heaven(s) |
| *unter freiem Himmel* | *in the open air* |
| *um Himmels willen!* | *for goodness' sake!* |
| *am Himmel* | *in the sky* |
| **hin** → her | there |
| *hin und wieder* | *every now and then, at times* |
| *hin und her* | *to and fro* |
| *(eine Fahrkarte) hin und zurück, Rückfahrkarte* | *(a) return (ticket)* |
| **hi'nauf** → herunter | upward(s) |
| *die Treppe hinauf* | *upstairs* |
| **hi'naus** → herein | out |
| *hinaus!* | *(get) out! out you go!* |
| *worauf wollen Sie hinaus?* | *what are you driving at?* |
| **hi'naus\|gehen i-a** | to go out, to leave |
| **'hindern** | to check, to prevent (from) |
| **hin'durch** | through; during |

| | |
|---|---|
| *den ganzen Tag hindurch* | *all day (long)* |
| *das ganze Jahr hindurch* | *all the year round* |
| **hi'nein** → heraus | in, into |
| **'hin\|fallen** ie-a/ä | to fall (down) |
| *der Länge nach hinfallen* | *to come down full length* |
| **'hin\|legen** | to lay/put down |
| *sich hinlegen* | *to lie down* |
| **'hinten** → vorn | behind |
| *nach hinten* | *backward(s)* |
| **'hintereinander** → nebeneinander | one after another |
| **'hinterher** → vorher | behind; after(wards) |
| **hi'nunter** → herauf | down(stairs) |
| *hinuntergehen* | *to go down(stairs)* |
| **hin'zu\|fügen** | to add |
| **die 'Hitze** → Kälte | heat |
| *hitzebeständig* | *heat-resistant* |
| **hoch** / höher / am höchsten → tief, niedrig | high; tall |
| *3 Meter hoch sein* | *to be 3 metres high/in height* |
| *Kopf hoch!* | *cheer up!* |
| *hochachtungsvoll* | *yours faithfully, yours sincerely* |
| *hochheben* | *to raise* |
| **höchst** | extremely |
| *höchst gefährlich* | *most dangerous* |
| **'höchstens** → mindestens / wenigstens | at (the) most |
| **der Hof** es/ö-e | court |
| *auf dem Hof* | *in the court(yard)* |
| **'hoffen** | to hope |
| *ich hoffe es* | *I hope so* |
| **'hoffentlich** | it is to be hoped; I hope, let's hope |
| **die 'Hoffnung** /en | hope |
| *in der Hoffnung* | *hoping (to)* |

| | |
|---|---|
| **'höflich** → unhöflich | polite |
| **die 'Höhe** /n → Tiefe | height |
| *in die Höhe werfen* | *to throw up* |
| *das ist die Höhe!* | *that's the limit!* |
| **hohl** | hollow |
| *ein hohler Baum* | *a hollow tree* |
| *die hohle Hand* | *the hollow of o's hand* |
| **'holen** | to call, to fetch |
| *holen lassen* | *to send for* |
| *holen Sie den Arzt!* | *call the doctor* |
| **das Holz** es/ö-er | wood |
| *aus Holz* | *(made) of wood* |
| *Holz hacken* | *to chop wood* |
| *ein Stück Holz* | *a piece of wood* |
| **der 'Honig** s | honey |
| **'hören** | to hear; to listen |
| *hören Sie mal!* | *I say!* |
| *hören Sie mal zu!* | *(just) listen!* |
| *ich höre (zu)* | *I am listening* |
| *er will nicht hören* | *he won't listen* |
| *ich habe gehört (, daß)* | *I hear (that)* |
| *eine Vorlesung hören* | *to attend a course/lecture* |
| *von sich hören lassen* | *to send word, to let know* |
| **der 'Hörer** s/- | listener; receiver |
| *den Hörer abnehmen / auflegen* | *to lift/replace the receiver* |
| **der 'Hörfunk** s | sound radio |
| **die 'Hose**(n) (pl) | trousers, pants |
| *eine Hose* | *a pair of trousers* |
| *Hosen tragen* | *to wear trousers* |
| *die Hosen anhaben* | *to wear the trousers* |
| **das Ho'tel** s/s | hotel |
| *im Hotel übernachten* | *to stay the night at a hotel* |
| **hübsch** → häßlich | pretty, nice; fine |
| *eine hübsche Geschichte!* | *a pretty mess!* |
| *das ist hübsch von dir* | *it is nice of you* |
| **der 'Hügel** s/- | hill |
| **das Huhn** s/ü-er | hen, chicken |

| | |
|---|---|
| **der Hund** es/e | dog |
| *Vorsicht! Bissiger Hund!* | *Beware of the dog. He bites* |
| *Hunde an der Leine führen!* | *Keep your dog on the lead* |
| *Mit Hunden kein Zutritt!* | *Dogs are not admitted* |
| **'hundert** | a/one hundred |
| *Hunderte (von)* | *hundreds (of)* |
| *zu Hunderten* | *by the hundred* |
| **der 'Hunger** s | hunger |
| *ich habe Hunger* | *I am hungry* |
| *ich habe keinen Hunger* | *I am not hungry* |
| **'hungrig** → satt | hungry |
| *ich bin hungrig* | *I am hungry* |
| **'husten** | to cough |
| *den Husten haben* | *to have a cough* |
| **der Hut** s/ü-e | hat |
| *einen Hut tragen* | *to wear a hat* |
| *den Hut aufsetzen* | *to put on o's hat* |
| *den Hut abnehmen* | *to take off o's hat* |
| *Hut ab!* | *hats off!* |
| **sich 'hüten (vor)** | to guard (against), to look out (for) |
| **die 'Hütte** /n | hut |
| *die Eisenhütte* | *iron and steel works* |

## I

| | |
|---|---|
| **ich** selbst | I myself |
| *ich bin's* | *it's me* |
| *hier bin ich* | *here I am* |
| *ich bin dran* | *it's my turn* |
| **ide'al** | ideal |
| **das Ide'al** s/e | ideal |
| **die I'dee** /n | idea |
| *das ist eine (gute) Idee* | *that's an idea, a good idea* |

| | |
|---|---|
| **'immer** → nie | always |
| *immer wieder* | *over and over again* |
| *immer besser* | *better and better* |
| *immer schlechter* | *worse and worse, from bad to worse* |
| *immer größer* | *bigger and bigger, ever bigger* |
| *immer noch* | *still* |
| **immer'hin** | after all |
| **die Indu'strie** /n | industry |
| *die Eisenindustrie* | *iron industry* |
| *die Elektroindustrie* | *electrical industry* |
| *industriell* | *industrial* |
| **der Inge'nieur** s/e | engineer |
| **der 'Inhalt** s/e | contents |
| *das Inhaltsverzeichnis* | *table of contents* |
| **'innen** → außen | within, inside |
| **'innere** → äußere | inner |
| *das Innere* | *interior, inside* |
| *im Innern* | *within, inside* |
| **das In'sekt** s/en | insect |
| **die 'Insel** /n | island; isle |
| *auf einer Insel* | *on an island* |
| **das Instru'ment** es/e | instrument |
| *ein Instrument spielen* | *to play an instrument* |
| **interes'sant** | interesting |
| *wie interessant!* | *how interesting!* |
| **das Inter'esse** s/n | interest |
| *Interesse haben (an, für)* | *to take an interest* (*in*), *to be interested in* |
| *ich habe (kein) Interesse (dafür)* | *I am* (*not*) *interested* (*in it*) |
| *es liegt in deinem Interesse* | *it's in your* (*own*) *interest* |
| **sich interes'sieren (für)** | to be interested (in) |
| **in'zwischen** | meanwhile |
| **'irgendein** (Buch) | some/any (book) |

| | |
|---|---|
| *irgend etwas* | *something (or other)/ anything* |
| *irgend jemand* | *somebody (or other)/ anybody* |
| *irgendwie* | *somehow (or other)/ anyhow* |
| *irgendwo(hin)* | *somewhere (or other)/ anywhere* |
| **'irren, sich irren** | to make a mistake |
| *sich im Weg irren* | *to go the wrong way* |
| *wenn ich (mich) nicht irre* | *if I'm not mistaken* |
| *da irren Sie sich* | *there you are mistaken* |
| **der 'Irrtum** s/ü-er | error, mistake |
| *im Irrtum sein* | *to be mistaken/wrong* |
| **ist** (3rd pers sg pres of **sein**) | is |
| **I'talien** s | Italy |

## J

| | |
|---|---|
| **ja** → nein | yes |
| *ja, gern* | *yes, I'd like to, thank you* |
| *ja doch! aber ja!* | *why, yes! yes, indeed!* |
| **die 'Jacke** /n | jacket |
| **die Jagd** /en | hunting/shooting |
| *Jagd machen (auf)* | *to hunt (for)* |
| *auf die Jagd gehen* | *to go hunting/shooting* |
| **'jagen** | to hunt |
| **der 'Jäger** s/- | hunter |
| **das Jahr** es/e | year |
| *im Jahre 1968* | *in 1968* |
| *dieses Jahr* | *this year* |
| *nächstes Jahr* | *next year* |
| *voriges Jahr* | *last year* |
| *alle Jahre* | *every year* |
| *vor einem Jahr* | *a year ago* |

| | |
|---|---|
| *ein halbes Jahr* | *half a year, six months* |
| *einmal im Jahr* | *once a year* |
| *3 Jahre jünger* | *3 years younger* |
| *sie ist 20 (Jahre)* | *she is 20 (years old)* |
| *mit 20 Jahren* | *at the age of 20* |
| **die 'Jahreszeit /en** | season |
| **das Jahr'hundert s/e** | century |
| **-jährig : 'zehnjährig** | 10 years old; lasting 10 years |
| **'jährlich** | yearly, every year |
| *einmal jährlich* | *once a year* |
| **'je(mals)** → nie | ever |
| *hat man je so was gesehen?* | *did you ever see such a thing?* |
| **je . . . 'desto** | the . . . the |
| *je mehr man hat, desto mehr man will* | *the more we have, the more we want* |
| **'jedenfalls** | in any case |
| **'jeder** → keiner | every/each; everybody/anybody |
| *ohne jeden Zweifel* | *without any doubt* |
| **'jedermann** → niemand | everybody, anybody |
| **'jedesmal** → keinmal | every/each time |
| *jedesmal, wenn* | *whenever* |
| **je'doch** / aber | yet, however |
| **'jemand** → niemand | somebody/anybody |
| *jemand anders* | *someone else* |
| *(ist) jemand hier?* | *(is) anybody there?* |
| *ohne jemand zu sehen* | *without seeing anybody* |
| **'jene(r,s)** | that; that one |
| **'jenseits** | on the other side |
| **jetzt** | now, at present |
| *bis jetzt* | *up to now, as yet* |
| *von jetzt (an)* | *from now on* |
| *eben jetzt* | *just now, this very instant* |
| **die 'Jugend** → Alter | youth |
| *von Jugend auf* | *from o's youth* |

| | |
|---|---|
| *die Jugendherberge* | *youth hostel* |
| **jung** / jünger / am jüngsten → alt | young |
| *die jungen Leute* pl | *young people* |
| *er ist 5 Jahre jünger als ich* | *he is 5 years younger than me/I* |
| **der 'Junge** n/n | boy |
| *Jungens!* pl | *lads!* |

## K

| | |
|---|---|
| **der 'Kaffee** s/s | coffee |
| *eine Tasse Kaffee* | *a cup of coffee* |
| *Kaffee kochen* | *to make (the) coffee* |
| *Kaffee trinken* | *to have coffee* |
| *zum Kaffee(trinken) einladen* | *to invite to (afternoon) coffee* |
| *einen Kaffee bestellen* | *to order a (cup of) coffee* |
| *Milchkaffee* | *white coffee* |
| *die Kaffeekanne* | *coffee pot* |
| **der Ka'kao** s | cocoa |
| **kalt** / kälter / am kältesten → warm / heiß | cold |
| *es ist kalt* | *it is cold* |
| *mir ist kalt* | *I am/feel cold* |
| **die 'Kälte** → Hitze / Wärme | cold |
| *es sind 10 Grad Kälte* | *it is 10 degrees below zero* |
| *vor Kälte zittern* | *to shiver with cold* |
| **kam** (1st, 3rd pers sg pret of **kommen**) | |
| **die 'Kamera** /s | camera |
| **der Kame'rad** en/en | comrade, fellow, companion |
| **der Kamm** s/ä-e | comb |

| | |
|---|---|
| *(sich) kämmen* | *to comb* |
| **der Kampf** es/ä-e | fight, struggle |
| *der Wettkampf* | *match* |
| **'kämpfen** | to fight, to struggle |
| **kann** (1st, 3rd pers sg pres of **können**) | |
| **das Kapi'tal** s/ien | capital |
| *Kapital schlagen aus* | *to profit by* |
| **der Kapi'tän** s/e | captain |
| **ka'putt** | broken, in pieces |
| **die 'Karte** /n | map; card; ticket |
| *die Karte von Deutschland* | *the map of Germany* |
| *Karten spielen* | *to play cards* |
| *eine Karte lösen* | *to buy a ticket* |
| **die Kar'toffel** /n | potato |
| **der 'Käse** s/- | cheese |
| **die 'Kasse** /n | cash-box; cash-desk; booking/box office |
| **der 'Kasten** s/ä | case, box |
| **die 'Katze** /n | cat |
| **'kauen** | to chew |
| **der Kauf** s/äu-e → Verkauf | purchase; bargain |
| *einen guten Kauf machen* | *to make a good buy* |
| **'kaufen** → verkaufen | to buy |
| *der Käufer* | *buyer* |
| *das Kaufhaus* | *stores* |
| *der Kaufmann* | *business man; tradesman* |
| **kaum** | scarcely, hardly |
| **'kehren** | to sweep; to turn |
| *jdm den Rücken kehren* | *to turn o's back on s.o.* |
| **'keine(r,s)** → jeder | no one, none |
| *keiner von beiden* | *neither* |
| *keinesfalls/keineswegs* | *not at all, by no means* |
| **der 'Keller** s/- | cellar |
| **'kennen** a-a | to know |
| *kennenlernen* | *to get to know, to meet* |

| | |
|---|---|
| **die 'Kenntnis** /se | knowledge |
| *zur Kenntnis nehmen* | *to take note* (*of*) |
| **der Kerl** s/e | fellow |
| *ein ganzer / tüchtiger Kerl* | *a splendid chap* |
| **das 'Kilo(gramm)** s/- | kilo(gram) |
| **der / das Kilo'meter** s/- | kilometre |
| **das Kind** es/er | child |
| **das 'Kino** s/s | cinema |
| *ins Kino gehen* | *to go to the pictures* |
| *im Kino* | *at the cinema/pictures* |
| **die 'Kirche** /n | church |
| *in die Kirche gehen* | *to go to church* |
| *in der Kirche* | *at church* |
| **die 'Kirsche** /n | cherry |
| **die 'Klage** /n | complaint |
| *(sich be)klagen (über)* | *to complain* (*of*) |
| **klar** → unklar | clear, bright |
| *na, klar!* | *obviously!* |
| *ein klarer Himmel* | *a clear sky* |
| *klares Wasser* | *clear/pure water* |
| *eine klare Antwort* | *a plain answer* |
| *das ist klar* | *that is understood* |
| *die Klarheit* | *clearness* |
| **die 'Klasse** /n | class |
| *eine Fahrkarte erster, zweiter Klasse* | *a first-class, second-class, ticket* |
| *das Klassenzimmer* | *classroom* |
| **'kleben** | to stick |
| *Ankleben verboten!* | *Post no bills* |
| *der Klebestreifen* | *adhesive tape* |
| **das Kleid** es/er | dress |
| *die Kleider* pl | *dresses; clothes* |
| *ein neues Kleid* | *a new dress* |
| **die 'Kleidung** /en; Kleidungsstücke | *clothes, clothing, wear* |
| **klein** → groß | little/small |
| *kleines Geld / Kleingeld* | (*small*) *change* |

| | |
|---|---|
| *die Kleinen* pl | *the little ones* |
| **'klettern** | to climb |
| *auf einen Baum klettern* | *to climb (up) a tree* |
| *auf einen Berg klettern* | *to scale a mountain* |
| **die 'Klinge** /n | blade |
| **die 'Klingel** /n | bell |
| *klingeln* | *to ring the bell* |
| *es klingelt* | *the bell is ringing* |
| **'klopfen** | to knock |
| *es klopft* | *there is a knock at the door* |
| *an die Tür klopfen* | *to knock at the door* |
| **klug** → dumm | clever, intelligent |
| *die Klugheit* | *cleverness, intelligence* |
| **das Knie** s/- | knee |
| *das Knie beugen* | *to bend o's knee* |
| *knien* | *to kneel* |
| **der 'Knochen** s/- | bone |
| **der Knopf** es/ö-e | button |
| *(auf) den Knopf drücken* | *to press the button* |
| **'kochen** | to boil; to cook; to do the cooking |
| *das Wasser kocht* | *the water is boiling* |
| *das Essen kochen* | *to cook the meal* |
| *Kaffee kochen* | *to make coffee* |
| *sie kocht gut* | *she is a good cook* |
| **der 'Koffer** s/- | (suit)case |
| *seine Koffer packen* | *to pack o's bags* |
| **die 'Kohle** /n | coal |
| *die Braunkohle* | *brown coal, lignite* |
| *die Steinkohle* | *hard coal* |
| **der Ko'llege** n/n | colleague |
| **'komisch** → ernst | funny; odd |
| *ein komischer Einfall* | *a funny idea* |
| *ein komischer Kerl* | *a queer fellow* |
| **'kommen** a-o → gehen | to come |
| *ich komme schon!* | *(I am) coming!* |
| *es kommt vor, daß* | *it happens that* |

| | |
|---|---|
| *wie kommt es, daß . . .?* | *how is it that . . .?* |
| *kommen lassen* | *to send for* |
| *spät kommen* | *to be late* |
| *zur Sache kommen* | *to come to the point* |
| *komm her!* | *come here!* |
| *kommen Sie morgen zu mir* | *come and see me tomorrow* |
| **die Konfe'renz** /en | conference |
| **'können** o-o/a | to be able (to); to know |
| *er kann seine Aufgabe* | *he knows his lesson* |
| *er kann Englisch* | *he can speak English* |
| *auswendig können* | *to know by heart* |
| *das kann sein* | *that may be* (so), *that's possible* |
| **das Kon'zert** s/e | concert |
| **der Kopf** es/ö-e | head |
| *sich den Kopf zerbrechen* | *to rack o's brains* |
| *er ist ein kluger Kopf* | *he has brains* |
| *aus dem Kopf* | *from memory, by heart* |
| *den Kopf schütteln* | *to shake o's head* |
| *die Kopfschmerzen* pl | *headache* |
| *Kopfschmerzen haben* | *to have* (*got*) *a headache* |
| **das Korn** s/ö-er | corn; grain |
| **der 'Körper** s/- | body |
| *der menschliche Körper* | *the human body* |
| *der Körperteil* | *part of the body* |
| **'kostbar** → wertlos | precious |
| **'kosten** | to cost; to taste |
| *viel kosten* | *to be expensive* |
| *was kostet das Buch?* | *how much is this book?* |
| *ich koste den Wein* | *I'll taste the wine* |
| **die 'Kosten** pl | cost(s) |
| *auf meine Kosten* | *at my expense* |
| *die Kosten tragen* | *to bear the costs* |
| *kostenlos* | *free of charge* |
| **die Kraft** /ä-e → Schwäche | strength, power |
| *in Kraft treten* | *to come into force* |

| | |
|---|---|
| *aus Leibeskräften* | *with all one's might* |
| **der 'Kraftfahrer** s/- | motorist, driver |
| **'kräftig** → schwach | strong |
| **krank** / kränker / kränkst → gesund | ill, sick |
| *schwer krank* | *sick* |
| *krank werden* | *to fall ill* |
| **der 'Kranke** n/n | patient |
| *einen Kranken pflegen* | *to nurse a patient* |
| **das 'Krankenhaus** es/äu-er | hospital |
| *ins Krankenhaus bringen* | *to take to the hospital* |
| *die Krankenschwester* | *nurse* |
| **die 'Krankheit** /en → Gesundheit | illness, sickness |
| *sich eine Krankheit zuziehen* | *to be taken ill* |
| **die 'Kreide** /n | chalk |
| **der Kreis** es/e | circle, ring |
| *im Kreise* | *in a circle* |
| *im Kreise der Familie* | *within the family* |
| *(der) Kreisverkehr* | *roundabout* |
| **das Kreuz** es/e | cross |
| *die Kreuzung* | *crossing* |
| **'kriechen** o-o | to creep |
| **der Krieg** s/e → Frieden | war |
| *im Krieg* | *at war* |
| *Krieg führen (gegen)* | *to make war* (*on*) |
| *der Zweite Weltkrieg* | *World War II* |
| **'kriegen** → geben | to get |
| **die Kri'tik** /en | criticism |
| *Kritik üben* | *to criticize* |
| **krumm** → gerade | curved; bent, crooked |
| *eine krumme Linie* | *a curved line* |
| *ein krummer Nagel* | *a bent nail* |
| **die 'Küche** /n | kitchen |
| **der 'Kuchen** s | cake |
| *einen Kuchen backen* | *to make a cake* |

| | |
|---|---|
| **die 'Kugel** /n | ball; bullet |
| *der Kugelschreiber* | *ball(-point) pen* |
| **die Kuh** /ü-e | cow |
| **kühl** → warm | cool |
| *es ist kühl* | *it is cool* |
| *der Kühlschrank* | *refrigerator* |
| **die Kul'tur** /en | culture, civilization |
| **der 'Kunde** n/n | customer |
| **die Kunst** /ü-e | art |
| *die schönen Künste* pl | *the fine arts* |
| *das ist keine Kunst* | *that's easy* |
| **der 'Künstler** s/- | artist |
| **das 'Kunstwerk** s/e | work of art |
| **der 'Kurs** es/e | course |
| *einen Kurs besuchen* | *to attend a course* |
| **die 'Kurve** /n | curve; bend |
| **kurz** → lang | short |
| *vor kurzem* | *recently, a short while ago* |
| *in / binnen kurzem* | *before long* |
| *kurz darauf* | *shortly after* |
| *kurz und gut* | *in short, in a word* |
| *Fasse dich kurz!* | *Make it short!* |
| **'kürzlich** | recently |
| **'küssen** | to kiss |
| **die 'Küste** /n | coast, shore |

## L

| | |
|---|---|
| **'lächeln (über)** | to smile (at) |
| *lächerlich* | *ridiculous* |
| **'lachen (über)** → weinen | to laugh (at) |
| *daß ich nicht lache!* | *don't make me laugh!* |
| *das ist nicht zum Lachen* | *it is no joke* |
| **der 'Laden** s/ä | shop |
| **die 'Ladung** /en | charge, load |

| | |
|---|---|
| **lag** (1st, 3rd pers sg pret of **liegen**) | |
| die '**Lage** /n | situation, position |
| *in der Lage sein (zu)* | *to be in a position (to)* |
| das '**Lager** s/- | couch; stock/store; camp |
| *auf Lager* | *in stock/store* |
| die '**Lampe** /n | lamp |
| das **Land** es/ä-er | land; country |
| *an Land gehen* | *to go ashore* |
| *auf dem Lande* | *in the country* |
| *zu Wasser und zu Lande* | *by land and by sea* |
| *die Landschaft* | *landscape* |
| die '**Landkarte** /n | map |
| die '**Landstraße** /n | road |
| der '**Landwirt** s/e | farmer |
| die '**Landwirtschaft** | farming, agriculture |
| '**landen** → starten | to land, to touch down |
| *die Landung* | *landing, touchdown* |
| **lang** → kurz | long |
| *2 Meter lang* | *2 metres long* |
| *2 Jahre lang* | *for 2 years* |
| *vor langer Zeit* | *long ago* |
| *seit langem* | *for a long time past* |
| *über kurz oder lang* | *sooner or later* |
| *stundenlang* | *for hours* |
| *die ganze Woche lang* | *all (the) week (long)* |
| '**lange** → kurz | (for) a long time |
| *wie lange?* | *how long?* |
| *schon lange* | *a long time since* |
| *wie lang schon?* | *how long?* |
| *(es ist) lange her* | *(it is a) long (time) ago* |
| *lange brauchen (um zu)* | *to take (a) long (time) (to)* |
| *die Langspielplatte* | *long playing record, LP* |
| die '**Länge** /n → Kürze | length |
| *der Länge nach* | *in length* |
| *sich in die Länge ziehen* | *to drag on (and on)* |
| *die Wellenlänge* | *wavelength* |

| | |
|---|---|
| **'langsam** → schnell | slow |
| *Langsamer fahren!* | *Slow down* |
| *immer langsam!* | *take it easy!* |
| **längst** | long ago/since |
| **das langt** | that'll do |
| **'langweilig** | boring, dull |
| **der 'Lappen** s/- | rag |
| **der Lärm** s | noise |
| *Lärm machen* | *to make a lot of noise* |
| **'lassen** ie-a/ä | to let; to make |
| *laß (das)!* | *don't! stop it!* |
| *laß mich in Ruhe!* | *leave me alone!* |
| *lassen Sie mich nur machen* | *leave that to me* |
| *holen lassen* | *to send for* |
| *machen lassen* | *to have done* |
| **die Last** /en | load |
| *eine schwere Last tragen* | *to carry a heavy load* |
| *das Lastauto, der LKW (Lastkraftwagen)* | *lorry, truck* |
| **der Lauf** s/äu-e | course; race; running |
| *im Laufe der Zeit* | *in the course of time* |
| *im Laufe dieser Woche* | *in the course of this week* |
| *den Lauf gewinnen* | *to win the race* |
| **'laufen** ie-au/äu | to run |
| *auf dem laufenden sein* | *to be up-to-date* |
| *der Motor läuft* | *the engine runs* |
| *das Wasser läuft* | *the water runs/flows* |
| **die 'Laune** /n | humour |
| *guter Laune sein* | *to be in a good humour/ in high spirits* |
| **laut** → leise / still | loud |
| *mit lauter Stimme* | *in a loud voice* |
| *laut sprechen* | *to speak loudly* |
| *lauter!* | *speak up!* |
| **'läuten** | to ring |
| *es läutet* | *the bell is ringing* |
| **'leben** → sterben | to live |
| *leben Sie wohl!* | *goodbye* |

| | |
|---|---|
| **das 'Leben** s → Tod | life |
| *am Leben sein* | *to be alive* |
| *am Leben bleiben* | *to remain alive* |
| *ums Leben kommen* | *to lose o's life* |
| **le'bendig** | living, alive; lively |
| *Lebensgefahr!* | *Danger* |
| *es ist lebensgefährlich (zu)* | *it is dangerous (to)* |
| **die 'Lebensmittel** pl | food, provisions |
| **'lebhaft** → ruhig | lively |
| *eine lebhafte Straße* | *a busy street* |
| **das 'Leder** s | leather |
| *aus Leder* | *made of leather* |
| **'ledig** → verheiratet | unmarried, single |
| **leer** → voll | empty |
| *leeren* | *to empty* |
| **'legen** | to lay, to put, to place |
| *sich (hin)legen* | *to lie down; to go to bed* |
| **die 'Lehre** /n | lesson; theory; science; teaching |
| **'lehren** | to teach |
| *Sprachen lehren* | *to teach languages* |
| *lesen lehren* | *to teach reading* |
| **der 'Lehrer** s/- | teacher, master |
| *mein alter Lehrer* | *my former teacher* |
| *Deutschlehrer* | *German master* |
| **der 'Lehrling** s/e | apprentice |
| **der Leib** es/er | body |
| *mit Leib und Seele* | *(with) heart and soul* |
| *Leibschmerzen haben* | *to have a stomach ache* |
| **leicht** → schwer, schwierig | light; easy |
| *ein leichter Fehler* | *a slight mistake* |
| *eine leichte Arbeit* | *an easy task* |
| *leicht gesagt!* | *it's easy to say that* |
| **das Leid** s/en → Freude | harm; sorrow |
| *es tut mir leid (daß)* | *I'm sorry (that)* |
| *er tut mir leid* | *I pity him, I'm sorry for him* |
| **'leiden i-i (an)** | to suffer (from) |

| | |
|---|---|
| *Hunger leiden* | *to suffer (from) hunger* |
| *Not leiden* | *to suffer want* |
| *ich kann ihn nicht leiden* | *I cannot stand him* |
| **die 'Leidenschaft** /en | passion |
| **'leider** → *glücklicherweise* | unfortunately; alas; afraid . . . |
| **'leihen** ie-ie | to lend; to borrow |
| *leihe mir das Buch* | *lend me the book* |
| *ich leihe es von ihm* | *I borrow it from him* |
| **'leise** → laut | quiet; soft |
| *leise!* | *be quiet! silence!* |
| *mit leiser Stimme* | *in a low voice* |
| *leise sprechen* | *to speak softly* |
| *leiser stellen* | *to turn lower* |
| **'leisten** | to do; to accomplish |
| *Hilfe leisten* | *to lend a (helping) hand* |
| *Widerstand leisten* | *to offer resistance (to)* |
| *einen Dienst leisten* | *to render a service* |
| **die 'Leiter** /n | ladder |
| *auf die Leiter steigen* | *to go up the ladder* |
| **die 'Leitung** /en | line; management |
| *die Leitung ist besetzt* | *the line is busy* |
| **'lernen** | to learn |
| *auswendig lernen* | *to learn by heart* |
| *Deutsch lernen* | *to learn German* |
| *lesen lernen* | *to learn to read* |
| **'lesen** a-e/ie | to read |
| *laut lesen* | *to read aloud* |
| *der Leser* | *reader* |
| **der / die / das 'letzte** | the last; the latest |
| *der vorletzte* | *the last but one* |
| *letztes Jahr* | *last year* |
| *letzten Sonntag* | *last Sunday* |
| **'leuchten** | to shine, to (give) light |
| **die 'Leute** pl | people |
| *gewisse Leute* | *certain people* |
| *die meisten Leute* | *most people* |
| *sehr viele Leute* | *a great many people* |

| | |
|---|---|
| *die jungen / alten Leute* | *young/old people* |
| **das Licht** s/er; e | light |
| *Licht machen* | *to switch the light on* |
| *das Licht ausmachen* | *to switch the light off* |
| **lieb** | dear |
| *es ist mir lieb (daß)* | *I am glad (that)* |
| *Lieber Herr X!* | *Dear Mr X,* |
| *lieb haben* | *to be fond of, to love* |
| **die 'Liebe** | love |
| *aus Liebe (zu)* | *for (the) love (of)* |
| **'lieben** | to love; to like |
| *sie lieben sich* | *they love one another* |
| **'liebenswürdig** | kind |
| **'lieber** (cf. gern) | rather |
| *ich habe lieber* | *I prefer* |
| *ich möchte lieber . . .* | *I would rather . . .* |
| *ich trinke lieber Kaffee* | *I prefer coffee, I'd rather have a coffee* |
| *ich stehe lieber* | *I prefer standing* |
| **am 'liebsten** (cf. **gern**) | |
| **das Lied** s/er | song |
| *ein Lied singen* | *to sing a song* |
| **lief** (1st, 3rd pers sg pret of **laufen**) | |
| **'liefern** | to deliver; to furnish |
| **'liegen** a-e | to be situated/ placed; to lie |
| *im Bett liegen* | *to be in bed* |
| *bleiben Sie liegen!* | *stay lying down* |
| *es liegt mir daran (daß)* | *it means a lot to me, I am anxious (that)* |
| *an wem liegt es?* | *whose fault is it?* |
| *das Zimmer liegt nach dem Garten* | *the room overlooks the garden* |
| **ließ** (1st, 3rd pers sg pret of **lassen**) | |
| **liest** (2nd, 3rd pers sg pres of **lesen**) | |

| | |
|---|---|
| **das Line'al** s/e | ruler |
| **die 'Linie** /n | line |
| *eine gerade Linie ziehen* | *to draw a straight line* |
| *in erster Linie* | *first of all, primarily* |
| **'linke(r,s)** → rechte(r,s) | left |
| *zur linken (Hand)* | *on the left* |
| **links** → rechts | on the left, to the left |
| *von links nach rechts* | *from left to right* |
| *links abbiegen* | *to turn left* |
| *links fahren* | *to drive on the left* |
| **die 'Lippe** /n | lip |
| **die 'Liste** /n | list |
| *eine Liste aufstellen* | *to draw up a list* |
| **das** / der **'Liter** s/- | litre |
| **die Litera'tur** /en | literature |
| **das Loch** s/ö-er | hole |
| *ein Loch graben* | *to dig a hole* |
| *ein Loch reißen (in)* | *to tear a hole (in)* |
| **der 'Löffel** s/- | spoon |
| *ein Löffel(voll)* | *a spoonful (of)* |
| **der Lohn** s/ö-e | pay; wages, salary |
| **das Los** es/e | lot |
| **los!** | go on! go ahead! let's go! here goes! |
| *los werden* | *to get rid of* |
| *was ist los?* | *what's the matter? what's the trouble? what's up?* |
| *was ist mit ihm los?* | *what's the matter with him?* |
| **'los\|lassen** → festhalten | to let go |
| **'lösen** / losmachen | to undo; to detach |
| *eine Karte lösen* | *to buy a ticket* |
| *eine Aufgabe lösen* | *to solve a problem* |
| *die Lösung* | *solution* |
| **die Luft** /ü-e | air |
| *an die Luft gehen* | *to take an airing* |

| | |
|---|---|
| *tief Luft holen* | *to take a deep breath* |
| *in die Luft fliegen* | *to be blown up* |
| **die 'Luftpost** | air mail |
| *mit Luftpost* | *by air mail* |
| **die 'Lüge** /n → Wahrheit | lie |
| *lügen* | *to lie, to tell a lie* |
| **die Lust** /ü-e | desire; joy |
| *Lust haben (zu)* | *to feel like* |
| *keine Lust haben* | *not to feel like* |
| *mit Lust und Liebe* | *with heart and soul* |
| **'lustig** → traurig | gay, merry |
| *sich lustig machen (über)* | *to make fun (of)* |

## M

| | |
|---|---|
| **'machen** | to make, to do |
| *das macht nichts* | *that doesn't matter; never mind* |
| *wieviel macht das?* | *how much is it?* |
| *das macht zusammen 5 Mark* | *that comes to 5 marks* |
| *was macht er?* | *what's he doing?* |
| *das macht man nicht* | *that isn't done* |
| *nichts zu machen!* | *nothing doing!* |
| *ich mache mir nichts daraus* | *I don't care about it* |
| *mach's gut!* | *cheerio!* |
| **die Macht** /ä-e | power, might |
| *das steht nicht in meiner Macht* | *that's beyond my power* |
| *an der Macht sein* | *to be in power* |
| *an die Macht kommen* | *to come (in)to power* |
| **'mächtig** | powerful |
| **das 'Mädchen** s/- | girl |
| **mag** (1st, 3rd pers sg pres of **mögen**) | |
| **der 'Magen** s/ä | stomach |

| | |
|---|---|
| **'mager** → fett | lean |
| **die 'Mahlzeit** /en | meal |
| *eine Mahlzeit halten* | *to have a meal* |
| *3 Mahlzeiten am Tag* | *3 meals a day* |
| **mal** | just |
| *sag mal!* | *I say; just tell me* |
| *denken Sie mal!* | *just think of it!* |
| *komm mal her!* | *(just) come here* |
| *rate mal!* | *just guess!* |
| **das Mal** s/e | time |
| *zum ersten Mal* | *for the first time* |
| *zum letzen Mal* | *for the last time* |
| *das nächste Mal* | *next time* |
| *voriges Mal* | *last time* |
| *wieviele Male?* | *how often?* |
| *einmal* | *once* |
| *zweimal* | *twice* |
| *dreimal* | *three times* |
| *5 mal 4 ist 20 (5 × 4 = 20)* | *5 times 4 are 20* |
| *ein für allemal* | *once and for all* |
| **'malen** | to paint |
| *der Maler* | *painter* |
| *die Malerei* | *painting* |
| **Ma'ma** /s | mummy |
| **man** | one; you, we, they; people |
| *man hat mir gesagt* | *I've been told* |
| *man kann nie wissen* | *you never can tell* |
| **'manche(r,s)** | many a |
| *manches Mal* | *many a time* |
| **'manchmal** | sometimes |
| **der' Mangel** s/ä | absence, want, lack |
| *aus Mangel an* | *for want/lack of* |
| *Mangel haben (an)* | *to be in want (of)* |
| **der Mann** es/ä-er | man; husband |
| *männlich* | *masculine; male* |
| **der 'Mantel** s/ä | coat; overcoat |

| | |
|---|---|
| *einen Mantel tragen* | *to wear a coat* |
| *den Mantel anziehen* | *to put on o's coat* |
| **die 'Mappe** /n | briefcase |
| **die Mark** /- | mark |
| *10 Mark* | *10 marks* |
| **die 'Marke** /n | make, mark, sign; stamp |
| **der Markt** s/ä-e | market |
| *auf dem Markt* | *in the market* |
| **der Marsch** s/ä-e | march |
| *marschieren* | *to march* |
| **die Ma'schine** /n | machine, engine |
| *(mit der) Maschine schreiben* | *to type* |
| **das Maß** es/e | measure(ment) |
| *nach Maß* | *made to measure* |
| *Maß nehmen* | *to take measurements* |
| *in hohem Maße* | *in a high degree* |
| **'mäßig** → unmäßig | moderate |
| **die 'Masse** /n | mass |
| **das Materi'al** s/ien | material |
| **die Ma'terie** /n | matter |
| **der Ma'trose** n/n | sailor |
| **die 'Mauer** /n | wall |
| *der Maurer* | *bricklayer* |
| **die Maus** /äu-e | mouse |
| **der Me'chaniker** s/- | mechanic |
| **die Medi'zin**; /en | medicine |
| **das Meer** es/e | sea |
| *am Meer* | *at the seaside* |
| *auf dem Meer* | *at sea* |
| **das Mehl** s/e | flour |
| **mehr** (cf. **viel**) → weniger | more (than) |
| *immer mehr* | *more and more* |
| *mehr oder weniger* | *more or less* |
| *nicht mehr* | *no more, no longer* |
| *nichts mehr* | *nothing more* |
| *niemand mehr* | *nobody else* |
| **'mehrere** | several |

| | |
|---|---|
| **'mehrmals** | several times |
| **'meinen** | to think, to mean |
| *was meinen Sie dazu?* | *what do you think of that?* |
| *man sollte meinen* | *one would think* |
| *wie Sie meinen!* | *as you like!* |
| **'meinetwegen** | because of me |
| *meinetwegen!* | *I don't mind* |
| **die 'Meinung** /en | opinion |
| *meiner Meinung nach* | *in my opinion* |
| *Ich bin Ihrer Meinung* | *I agree with you* |
| *ich bin anderer Meinung* | *I'm of a different opinion* |
| *seine Meinung ändern* | *to change o's mind* |
| **'meist(ens)** | mostly, for the most part |
| *am meisten* | *most (of all)* |
| *die meisten Leute* | *most people* |
| **der 'Meister** s/- | master; champion |
| **'melden** | to announce; to report |
| *sich melden (bei)* | *to present o.s. (at)* |
| *sich (telefonisch) melden* | *to answer the telephone* |
| **die Melo'die** /n | melody, tune, air |
| **die 'Menge** /n | crowd, mass; quantity |
| *eine Menge von . . .* | *lots/plenty of . . .* |
| *in großen Mengen* | *in great quantities* |
| **der Mensch** en/en | man, person |
| *der gesunde Menschenverstand* | *common sense* |
| *Mensch!* | *man (alive)!, boy!* |
| **die 'Menschheit** | humanity, mankind |
| *menschlich* | *human* |
| *die Menschlichkeit* | *humanity* |
| **merken** | to notice, to observe |
| *sich merken* | *to make a note of* |
| **'merkwürdig** | curious, remarkable |
| **die 'Messe** /n | fair |

| | |
|---|---|
| **'messen** a-e/i | to measure |
| das **'Messer** s/- | knife |
| das **Me'tall** s/e | metal |
| das / der **'Meter** s/- | metre |
| *2 Meter breit / lang / hoch* | *2 metres wide/long/high* |
| der **'Metzger** s/- (cf. **Fleischer**) | butcher |
| **'mieten** | to rent, to hire |
| *zu vermieten* | *to let* |
| *Autovermietung* | *car hire* |
| die **Milch** | milk |
| die **Milli'on** /en | million |
| *2 Millionen Mark* | *2 million marks* |
| **'mindestens** → höchstens | at least |
| der **Mi'nister** s/- | minister |
| die **Mi'nute** /n | minute |
| *auf die Minute* | *to the minute* |
| **'mischen** | to mix |
| *die Mischung* | *mixture* |
| **miß'lingen** a-u → gelingen | to fail |
| **'mißverstehen** a-a → verstehen | to mistake, to misunderstand |
| der **Mist** es | muck |
| **'mit\|bringen** a-a | to bring (with one) |
| **'miteinander** → gegeneinander | with each other |
| das **'Mitglied** s/er | member |
| das **'Mitleid** s | pity |
| *aus Mitleid (für)* | *out of pity (for)* |
| *Mitleid haben (mit)* | *to have pity (on)* |
| **'mit\|nehmen** a-o/i | to take along |
| der **'Mittag** s/e | midday, noon |
| *zu Mittag* | *at midday/noon* |
| *gegen Mittag* | *towards midday/noon* |
| *heute mittag* | *at midday/noon today* |
| *das Mittagessen* | lunch |
| *(zu) Mittag essen* | *to have lunch* |
| *mittags* | *at noon* |

| | |
|---|---|
| **die 'Mitte** /n | middle, centre |
| *in der Mitte* | *in the middle* |
| *Mitte August* | *in mid-August* |
| **'mit\|teilen** | to make known, to communicate |
| **das 'Mittel** s/- | means; remedy |
| *Mittel und Wege finden* | *to find ways and means* |
| **der 'Mittelpunkt** s/e | centre |
| **'mitten (in)** | in the middle (of) |
| **(die) 'Mitternacht** | midnight |
| *um Mitternacht* | *at midnight* |
| **das 'Möbel** s/- | (piece of) furniture |
| **'möchte** (1st, 3rd pers sg cond of **mögen**) | would like (to) |
| **die 'Mode** /n | fashion |
| *nach der (neuesten) Mode* | *according to the* (*latest*) *fashion* |
| **mo'dern** | modern, up-to-date |
| **'mögen** o-o/a | to want, to like |
| *ich möchte (gern)* | *I should like* (*to*) |
| *ich möchte lieber* | *I would rather* |
| *ich möchte (gern) wissen* | *I wonder, I should like to know* |
| *was möchten Sie?* | *what do you want? what can I do for you?* |
| *das mag sein* | *that may be* |
| **'möglich** → unmöglich | possible |
| *das ist (wohl) möglich* | *that's* (*quite*) *possible* |
| *so bald wie möglich* | *as soon as possible* |
| *so oft wie möglich* | *as often as possible* |
| *so schnell wie möglich, möglichst schnell* | *as quickly as possible* |
| *sein möglichstes tun* | *to do o's best* |
| *es möglich machen (zu)* | *to make it possible* (*to*) |
| **die 'Möglichkeit** /en | possibility |
| **der Mo'ment** s/e | moment |
| *Moment, bitte!* | *just a moment, please!* |
| **der 'Monat** s/e | month |

|  |  |
|---|---|
| *der Monat Mai* | *the month of May* |
| *im (Monat) Mai* | *in May* |
| *am Ersten des Monats* | *on the first of the month* |
| *monatlich* | *monthly* |
| **der Mond** s/e | moon |
| *der Mond scheint / es ist Mondschein* | *the moon is shining* |
| **der Mord** s/e | murder |
| **'morgen** | tomorrow |
| *morgen früh* | *tomorrow morning* |
| *morgen mittag* | *(at) midday/noon tomorrow* |
| *morgen abend* | *tomorrow night/evening* |
| *übermorgen* | *the day after tomorrow* |
| *bis morgen!* | *see you tomorrow!* |
| *morgen in 8 Tagen* | *tomorrow week* |
| **der 'Morgen** s | morning |
| *am Morgen* | *in the morning* |
| *am frühen Morgen* | *early in the morning* |
| *vom Morgen bis zum Abend* | *from morning till night* |
| *heute morgen* | *this morning* |
| *gestern morgen* | *yesterday morning* |
| *am folgenden Morgen* | *the following morning* |
| *guten Morgen!* | *good morning* |
| *eines (schönen) Morgens* | *one of these (fine) days* |
| **'morgens** | in the morning |
| *um 5 Uhr morgens* | *at 5 o'clock in the morning* |
| *frühmorgens* | *early in the morning* |
| **der 'Motor** s/en | motor; engine |
| *den Motor anlassen* | *to start the engine* |
| *den Motor abstellen* | *to switch off the engine* |
| **das 'Motorrad** s/ä-er | motor-cycle |
| *Motorrad fahren* | *to ride a motor-cycle* |
| **die 'Mücke** /n | gnat |
| **'müde** | tired |

| | |
|---|---|
| *müde werden* | *to get tired* |
| *müde sein* | *to be tired* |
| *ich bin es müde* | *I have had enough of it* |
| **die 'Mühe** /n | trouble, pains |
| *mit großer Mühe* | *with great difficulty* |
| *Mühe haben (mit)* | *to have some trouble (with)* |
| *Mühe machen* | *to give trouble* |
| *sich die Mühe machen* | *to take the trouble* (*to*) |
| *sich Mühe geben* | *to take pains* |
| *es ist der Mühe wert* | *it's worth the trouble* |
| **die 'Mühle** /n | mill |
| **der Mund** s/ü-er | mouth |
| *halt den Mund!* | *shut up! be quiet!* |
| *von der Hand in den Mund leben* | *to live from hand to mouth* |
| *ein Mundvoll* | *a mouthful* |
| **die 'Mündung** /en | orifice; estuary |
| **die Mu'sik** | music |
| *Musik machen* | *to make music* |
| **der 'Muskel** s/n | muscle |
| **'müssen** | to be to, to have (got) to |
| *ich muß fort* | *I must go/be off* |
| *ich muß weggehen* | *I must be off/going* |
| *man muß arbeiten* | *one has to work* |
| **das 'Muster** s/- | model; sample |
| **der Mut** s → Angst | courage |
| *nur Mut!* | *cheer up!* |
| *den Mut verlieren* | *to lose courage* |
| *Mut fassen* | *to take courage/heart* |
| *guten Mutes sein* | *to be of good cheer* |
| **die 'Mutter** /ü | mother |
| *die Muttersprache* | *mother tongue* |
| **die 'Mütze** /n | cap |
| *die Mütze abnehmen / absetzen* | *to take off o's cap* |

## N

| | |
|---|---|
| **na!** | well! |
| *na so was!* | *well I never!* |
| **nach und nach** | little by little, bit by bit, gradually |
| **der 'Nachbar** n/n | neighbour |
| **'nach\|denken** a-a **(über)** | to think about, to reflect on |
| **'nacheinander** → gleichzeitig | one after another |
| **die 'Nachfrage** /n | demand |
| *Angebot und Nachfrage* | *supply and demand* |
| **'nach\|gehen** → vorgehen | to be slow |
| *die Uhr geht 5 Minuten nach* | *the clock is 5 minutes slow* |
| **'nachher** → vorher | after(wards) |
| **der 'Nachmittag** s/e | afternoon |
| *am Nachmittag / nachmittags* | *in the afternoon; p.m.* |
| *heute nachmittag* | *this afternoon* |
| *am frühen Nachmittag* | *in the early afternoon* |
| *am späten Nachmittag* | *in the late afternoon* |
| *um 5 Uhr nachmittags* | *at 5 in the afternoon* |
| **die 'Nachricht** /en | news |
| *die neuesten Nachrichten* | *the latest news* |
| *eine frohe Nachricht* | *a piece of good news* |
| *Nachricht haben (von)* | *to have word (from)* |
| **'nach\|sehen** a-e/ie | to check |
| **'nächste(r,s)** (cf. nahe) | next |
| *wer ist der nächste!* | *who comes next?* |
| *das nächste Mal* | *(the) next time* |
| *nächsten Sonntag* | *next Sunday* |
| *nächste Woche* | *next week* |
| *nächstes Jahr* | *next year* |
| **die Nacht** /ä-e | night |
| *eines Nachts* | *one night* |
| *gute Nacht!* | *good night* |

| | |
|---|---|
| *in der Nacht* | *in the night* |
| *die ganze Nacht* | *all night* |
| *heute nacht* | *tonight* |
| *über Nacht bleiben, übernachten* | *to stay overnight* |
| *es wird Nacht* | *it's getting dark* |
| *nachts* | *at night* |
| **nackt** | naked, bare |
| **die 'Nadel** /n | pin; needle |
| *die Sicherheitsnadel* | *safety pin* |
| *die Haarnadel* | *hairpin* |
| **der 'Nagel** s/ä | nail |
| **'nahe (bei)** / näher, am nächsten → fern | near, close by |
| *von nah und fern* | *from far and near* |
| **'nahezu** | nearly |
| **die 'Nähe** → Ferne | neighbourhood |
| *aus der Nähe* | *from close to* |
| *(ganz) in der Nähe* | *close by, nearby* |
| **'nähen** | to sew |
| *einen Knopf annähen* | *to sew on a button* |
| **nahm** (1st, 3rd pers sg pret of **nehmen**) | took |
| **die 'Nahrung** | food |
| **der 'Name** ns/n | name |
| *mein Name ist . . .* | *my name is . . .* |
| *wie ist Ihr Name?* | *what is your name?* |
| *der Vorname* | *Christian name* |
| *der Familienname* | *surname* |
| **'namentlich** | by name; particularly |
| **'nämlich** | namely, that is (to say) |
| **der Narr** en/en | fool |
| *zum Narren halten* | *to make a fool (of)* |
| **die 'Nase** /n | nose |
| *sich die Nase putzen* | *to blow o's nose* |
| *immer der Nase nach* | *just follow your nose* |
| **naß** → trocken | wet |
| *naß werden* | *to get wet* |

| | |
|---|---|
| **die Nati'on** /en | nation |
| *die Vereinten Nationen* | *the United Nations* |
| *national* | *national* |
| **die Na'tur** /en | nature |
| *von Natur aus* | *by nature* |
| *die Naturwissenschaft* | *natural science* |
| **na'türlich** | naturally, of course |
| **der 'Nebel** s/- | mist, fog |
| *es ist Nebel* | *it is misty/foggy* |
| **neben'an** | close by; next door |
| **'neben'bei** | by the way; besides |
| **'nebeneinander** → hintereinander | side by side |
| **'nehmen** a-o/i | to take |
| *den Bus nehmen* | *to take the bus* |
| *ein Bad nehmen* | *to have a bath* |
| *seine Arznei nehmen* | *to take o's medicine* |
| *da, nehmen Sie!* | (*there*), *take it!* |
| **der Neid** s | envy; jealousy |
| **'neigen** | to bend, to incline |
| **nein** → ja | no |
| *aber nein!* | *why, no!* |
| *mit nein antworten* | *to say no* |
| **'nennen** a-a | to call |
| *sich nennen* | *to be called* |
| **der Nerv** s/en | nerve |
| *auf die Nerven gehen* | *to get on s.o'.s nerves* |
| **nett** | nice, kind |
| *das ist nett von dir* | *that's nice of you* |
| *er ist nett zu ihnen* | *he is nice to them* |
| *wie nett!* | *how nice!* |
| **das Netz** es/e | net |
| *das Einkaufsnetz* | *string bag* |
| **neu** | new |
| *von neuem* | *newly* |
| *was Neues?* | *anything new?* |
| *das ist mir neu* | *that's news to me* |
| *was gibt es Neues?* | *what's the latest news?* |

| | |
|---|---|
| **die 'Neugier** | curiosity |
| *aus Neugier* | *out of curiosity* |
| **die 'Neuheit** /en | novelty |
| *die letzten Neuheiten* | *the latest novelties* |
| **die 'Neuigkeit** /en | (piece of) news |
| *eine Neuigkeit erfahren* | *to hear a piece of news* |
| **'neulich** | the other day, recently |
| **nicht** | not |
| *noch nicht* | *not yet* |
| *überhaupt nicht* | *not at all* |
| *warum nicht?* | *why not?* |
| *auch nicht* | *not . . . either* |
| *nicht wahr?* | *isn't it?* |
| *Nichtraucher* | *non-smoker; "No smoking"* |
| **nichts** → alles | nothing |
| *gar nichts* | *nothing at all* |
| *nichts anderes* | *nothing else* |
| *nichts mehr* | *no more* |
| *das macht nichts* | *it does not matter* |
| *(da ist) nichts zu machen* | (*there is*) *nothing to be done* (*about it*) |
| **nie** → immer | never |
| *nie wieder* | *never again* |
| **'nieder** → auf | down |
| *auf und nieder* | *up and down* |
| *nieder mit . . .!* | *down with . . .!* |
| **'niedrig** → hoch | low |
| **'niemals** → immer | never |
| **'niemand** → alle | nobody/no one |
| *niemand anders* | *nobody else* |
| *es ist niemand da* | *there is nobody there* |
| *ich habe niemanden gesehen* | *I didn't see anybody* |
| **nimmt** (3rd pers sg pres of **nehmen**) | |
| **'nirgends** / nirgendwo | nowhere, not anywhere |
| **noch** | still |

| | |
|---|---|
| *noch einmal* | *once again* |
| *noch nicht* | *not yet* |
| *noch etwas?* | *anything else?* |
| *noch einmal so viel* | *twice as much* |
| *noch heute* | *this very day* |
| *noch ein Brot* | *another loaf (of bread)* |
| *weder . . . noch* | *neither . . . nor* |
| *noch mal, nochmals* | *once again; once more* |
| **der 'Norden** s | north |
| *gegen Norden* | *to the north* |
| *im Norden (von)* | *in/to the north (of)* |
| *nördlich* | *north of; northern* |
| *die Nordseite* | *the northern side* |
| **nor'mal** | normal |
| **die Not** /ö-e | need; misery; danger |
| *zur Not* | *if need be* |
| *in Not sein* | *to be in need/danger* |
| *in Not geraten* | *to get into difficulties* |
| *Notausgang* | *Emergency exit* |
| *Notrufe* | *emergency calls* |
| **'nötig** → unnötig | necessary |
| *nötig haben* | *to be in need (of)* |
| *es ist nicht nötig* | *there is no need* |
| **'notwendig** | necessary |
| **die Null** /en | zero |
| *über / unter Null* | *above/below zero* |
| *zwei (zu) null* | *two goals to nil* |
| **die 'Nummer** /n | number |
| *die Nummer wählen* | *to dial the number* |
| *numerieren* | *to number* |
| **nun** | now |
| *nun!* | *why! well!* |
| *und nun?* | *well then?* |
| *was nun?* | *what next?* |
| **nur** / bloß | only |
| *nur noch 2 Minuten* | *only 2 minutes left* |
| *nicht nur . . ., sondern auch* | *not only . . ., but also* |

| | |
|---|---|
| **der 'Nutzen** s → Schaden | profit, use |
| *Nutzen ziehen (aus)* | *to profit (from)* |
| **'nützen** → schaden | to be useful |
| *es nützt nichts* | *it's no use* |
| 'nützlich | useful |

## O

| | |
|---|---|
| ob | whether |
| *als ob* | *as if, as though* |
| *(so) tun, als ob* | *to pretend (to)* |
| *und ob!* | *rather! and how!* |
| **'oben** → unten | above, up |
| *von oben* | *from above* |
| *von oben bis unten* | *from top to bottom* |
| *siehe oben* | *see above* |
| *da oben* | *up there* |
| *oben auf dem Berg* | *at the top of the mountain* |
| *oben auf dem Wasser* | *on the surface of the water* |
| **'obere** (r,s) → untere | upper, superior |
| die **'Oberfläche** /n | surface |
| das **Obst** es | fruit |
| der **'Ochse** n/n | ox |
| der **'Ofen** s/Ö | stove; oven |
| **'offen** → zu, geschlossen | open |
| *halb offen* | *half-open* |
| *offen gestanden* | *frankly speaking* |
| **'öffentlich** | public |
| *öffentlich bekanntmachen* | *to make public* |
| *die öffentliche Bekanntmachung* | *announcement* |
| *in der Öffentlichkeit* | *in public* |
| **'öffnen** → (ab/zu)schließen / zumachen | to open |
| *Hier öffnen!* | *Open here* |

| | |
|---|---|
| *geöffnet von . . . bis* | *open from . . . to* |
| **oft** / öfter / am öftsten → selten | often |
| *wie oft?* | *how often?* |
| *so oft wie möglich* | *as often as possible* |
| **oh!** das ist schön! | oh! that's lovely! |
| *o ja!* | *oh yes!* |
| *o nein!* | *oh no!* |
| **das Ohr** s/en | ear |
| **das Öl** s/e | oil |
| *in Öl* | *in oil*(*s*) |
| *die Ölheizung* | *oil heating* |
| **der 'Omnibus** ses/se | (motor-)bus; motor coach |
| **der 'Onkel** s/- | uncle |
| **die Operati'on** /en | operation |
| **das 'Opfer** s/- | sacrifice; victim |
| *ein Opfer bringen* | *to make a sacrifice* |
| *zum Opfer fallen* | *to fall a victim* (*to*) |
| **'ordnen** → verwirren | to put in order; to arrange |
| **die 'Ordnung** /en | order |
| *in Ordnung!* | *all right!* |
| *in Ordnung bringen* | *to put in order* |
| *ordentlich* | *tidy* |
| **der Ort** s/e | place |
| *an Ort und Stelle* | *on the spot* |
| *das Ortsgespräch* | *local call* |
| **der 'Osten** s | east |
| *im Osten (von)* | *in/to the east* (*of*) |
| *östlich* | *east of; eastern* |
| *die Ostseite* | *the eastern side* |
| **'Ostern** | Easter |
| *zu Ostern* | *at Easter* |
| *Fröhliche Ostern!* | *Happy Easter!* |
| **der 'Ozean** s/e | ocean |
| *der Ozeandampfer* | *ocean liner* |

# P

| | |
|---|---|
| **das Paar** s/e | pair; couple |
| *ein Paar Schuhe* | *a pair of shoes* |
| *paarweise* | *in pairs* |
| **ein paar** | a few |
| *vor ein paar Tagen* | *the other day* |
| *ein paarmal* | *several times* |
| **packen** | to pack; to seize |
| *den Koffer packen* | *to pack o's trunks* |
| *am Arm packen* | *to seize by the arm* |
| *Packpapier* | *wrapping paper* |
| *das Paket* | *parcel* |
| **die 'Panne** /n | breakdown |
| *Panne haben* | *to have a breakdown* |
| **das Pa'pier** s/e | paper |
| *ein Blatt Papier* | *a sheet of paper* |
| *Briefpapier* | *notepaper* |
| *Toilettenpapier* | *toilet-paper* |
| **der Park** s/s | park |
| **'parken** | to park |
| *Parken verboten!* | *No parking* |
| *der Parkplatz* | *parking place, car park* |
| **die Par'tei** /en | party |
| *Partei ergreifen* | *to take s.o.'s part* |
| *die führende Partei* | *the ruling party* |
| **der Paß** sses/ässe | passport |
| *die Paßkontrolle* | *passport control* |
| **'passen** | to fit |
| *der Mantel paßt (mir)* | *the coat fits me* |
| *das paßt sich nicht* | *that's not done* |
| *das paßt mir gut* | *that suits me well* |
| *das ist das passende Wort* | *that's the right word* |
| **pas'sieren** | to happen |
| **der Pati'ent** en/en | patient |
| **die 'Pause** /n | pause; break; interval |
| **die Per'son** /en | person, character |
| *ich für meine Person* | *as for me* |

| | |
|---|---|
| *der Personalausweis* | *identity card* |
| **per'sönlich** | personal |
| **die 'Pfeife** /n | whistle; pipe |
| *Pfeife rauchen* | *to smoke o's pipe* |
| **'pfeifen** i-i | to whistle |
| **der 'Pfennig** s/e | (penny) |
| **das Pferd** s/e | horse |
| *zu Pferde* | *on horseback* |
| **die 'Pflanze** /n | plant |
| **'pflanzen** | to plant |
| **'pflegen** | to take care (of), to nurse |
| *einen Kranken pflegen* | *to look after a patient* |
| **die Pflicht** /en | duty |
| *es ist meine Pflicht (zu)* | *it's my duty (to)* |
| **'pflücken** | to pick, to gather |
| **der Pflug** s/ü-e | plough |
| *pflügen* | *to plough* |
| **das Pfund** s/e | pound |
| *2 Pfund Brot* | *2 pounds of bread* |
| **die Phanta'sie** /n | imagination |
| **der 'Pinsel** s/- | brush |
| **der Plan** s/ä-e | plan |
| *einen Plan entwerfen* | *to make a plan* |
| *einen Plan ausführen* | *to carry out a plan* |
| **der Platz** es/ä-e | place |
| *Platz machen (für)* | *to make room (for)* |
| *Platz nehmen* | *to take a seat* |
| *bitte, nehmen Sie Platz* | *please sit down* |
| *einen Platz besetzen* | *to occupy a seat* |
| **'platzen** | to burst |
| *der Reifen ist geplatzt* | *the tyre has burst* |
| **'plötzlich** | all at once, suddenly |
| **die Poli'tik** | politics |
| **po'litisch** | political |
| *der Politiker* | *politician* |
| *über Politik sprechen* | *to talk politics* |
| **die Poli'zei** | police |

| | |
|---|---|
| *sich der Polizei melden* | *to report to the police* |
| *die Polizei rufen* | *to call for the police* |
| **der Poli'zist** en/en | policeman |
| **die Post** | post; post-office; mail |
| *die Post erledigen* | *to answer the mail* |
| *zur Post bringen* | *to post* |
| *mit der Post* | *by post* |
| *die Postkarte* | *postcard* |
| *postlagernd* | *to be called for, poste restante* |
| *postwendend* | *by return of post* |
| **der 'Posten** s/- | post |
| **'praktisch** | practical |
| **der Präsi'dent** en/en | president |
| **der Preis** es/e | price; prize |
| *um jeden Preis* | *at any price* |
| *um keinen Preis* | *not at any price* |
| *zum Preise von* | *at the price of* |
| *der Preis ist . . .* | *the price is . . .* |
| *einen Preis gewinnen* | *to win a prize* |
| **die 'Presse** /n | press |
| **'prima!** | marvellous! wonderful! |
| **pri'vat** | private |
| **das Pro'blem s/e** | problem |
| **das Pro'dukt s/e** | product |
| *produzieren* | *to turn out* |
| **das Pro'gramm** s/e | program(me) |
| **das Pro'zent s/e** | per cent |
| *zu wieviel Prozent?* | *at how much per cent?* |
| **'prüfen** | to examine; to test |
| **die 'Prüfung** /en | exam(ination); test |
| *eine Prüfung machen* | *to go in for an examination* |
| **das 'Publikum** s | public |
| **das Pult** s/e | desk; chair |
| **der Punkt** s/e | point; full stop |
| *Punkt für Punkt* | *point by point* |
| *in diesem Punkt* | *in this respect* |

| | |
|---|---|
| *Punkt 12 (Uhr)* | *at 12 (o'clock) sharp* |
| *ein wunder Punkt* | *a sore point* |
| **'pünktlich** → unpünktlich | punctual |
| *pünktlich sein* | *to be on time* |
| **'putzen** | to clean |
| *die Zähne putzen* | *to brush o's teeth* |
| *(sich) die Nase putzen* | *to blow o's nose* |
| *putz deine Schuhe* | *clean your shoes* |

## Q

| | |
|---|---|
| **die Quali'tät** /en | quality |
| **die Quanti'tät** /en | quantity |
| **die 'Quelle** /n | spring, source |
| *aus guter Quelle* | *on good authority* |
| *die Stromquelle* | *source of (electric) power* |
| **quer** über | across |
| *kreuz und quer* | *this way and that* |

## R

| | |
|---|---|
| **das Rad** s/ä-er | wheel; bicycle, bike |
| *radfahren* | *to ride a bicycle* |
| *der Radfahrer* | *cyclist* |
| **das 'Radio** s/s | radio, wireless, radio (set) |
| *im Radio* | *on the radio* |
| *Radio hören* | *to listen to the radio* |
| *im Radio hören* | *to hear on the radio* |
| *stell das Radio an!* | *turn on the radio* |
| *stell das Radio ab!* | *turn off the radio* |
| *der Radioapparat* | *radio/wireless set* |
| **die Ra'kete** /n | rocket |
| *eine Rakete abschießen* | *to launch a rocket* |
| **rasch** → langsam | quick |
| **sich ra'sieren** | to shave, to have a shave |
| *rasieren, bitte!* | *a shave, please!* |
| *der Rasierapparat* | *razor* |

| | |
|---|---|
| **der Rat** s/Ratschläge | advice |
| *einen guten Rat geben* | *to give a good piece of advice* |
| *um Rat fragen* | *to ask s.o.'s advice* |
| *höre auf seinen Rat* | *take his advice* |
| *ich werde seinen Rat befolgen* | *I'll follow his advice* |
| *das Rathaus* | *town hall/city hall* |
| **'raten** ie-a/ä | to advise; to guess |
| *rate mal!* | *just guess!* |
| *das Rätsel* | *mystery; puzzle* |
| *das ist mir ein Rätsel* | *that puzzles me* |
| **der Rauch** s | smoke |
| **'rauchen** | to smoke |
| *Rauchen verboten!* | *No smoking* |
| *der Raucher* | *smoker* |
| *Raucher(abteil)* | *smoking compartment* |
| *der Nichtraucher* | *non-smoker* |
| *Nichtraucher(abteil)* | *non-smoking compartment* |
| **der Raum** s/äu-e | room; space |
| *die Räume des Hauses* | *the rooms of the house* |
| *der Raumflug* | *space-flight* |
| **raus!** (cf. **heraus**) | |
| **'rechnen** | to reckon, to calculate; to count |
| **die 'Rechnung** /en | account; bill; invoice |
| *Ober, die Rechnung bitte!* | *waiter, the bill, please!* |
| *die Hotelrechnung* | *hotel bill* |
| **das Recht** s/e | right |
| *mit Recht* | *justly, with good reason, rightly* |
| *das Recht haben (zu)* | *to have the right* (*to*) |
| **recht** → unrecht | right |
| *zur rechten Zeit / rechtzeitig* | *in good time* |
| **recht haben** | to be right |
| *nicht recht haben* | *to be wrong* |

| | |
|---|---|
| **'rechte(r,s)** → linke(r,s) | right |
| *die rechte Hand* | *the right hand* |
| *zur rechten (Hand)* | *on the right* |
| **rechts** → links | on/to the right |
| *von rechts nach links* | *from right to left* |
| *rechts abbiegen* | *to turn right* |
| *rechts fahren* | *to drive on the right* |
| *rechts halten!* | *Keep right* |
| **die 'Rede** /n | speech |
| *eine Rede halten (über)* | *to make/deliver a speech (on)* |
| *das ist nicht der Rede wert* | *that's not worth mentioning* |
| **'reden** → schweigen | to talk |
| *mit jdm reden* | *to talk to s.o.* |
| *über etwas reden* | *to talk about sth.* |
| *über Politik reden* | *to talk politics* |
| *der Redner* | *speaker, orator* |
| **die 'Regel** /n → Ausnahme | rule |
| *in der Regel* | *as a rule* |
| *regelmäßig* | *regular* |
| **'regeln** | to regulate |
| **sich 'regen** | to stir; to be active |
| **der 'Regen** s/- | rain |
| *der Regenmantel* | *raincoat* |
| *der Regenschirm* | *umbrella* |
| *regnen* | *to rain* |
| *es regnet* | *it is raining* |
| *es regnet in Strömen* | *it's pouring with rain* |
| **die Re'gierung** /en | government |
| **'reiben** ie-ie | to rub |
| **reich** → arm | rich |
| *der Reichtum* | *wealth* |
| **'reichen** | to give, to pass; to suffice |
| *das reicht!* | *that will do, that's enough* |
| *die Hand reichen* | *to shake hands (with)* |

| | |
|---|---|
| *reichen Sie mir bitte das Salz!* | *will you pass me the salt, please* |
| **reif** → unreif | ripe |
| *reif werden* | *to ripen* |
| **der 'Reifen** s/- | tyre |
| *eine Reifenpanne haben* | *to have a flat tyre* |
| **die 'Reihe** /n | row; rank; series; line; file |
| *in einer Reihe* | *in a line/file* |
| *der Reihe nach* | *one after the other; in turn, by turns* |
| *wer ist an der Reihe?* | *whose turn is it?* |
| *ich bin an der Reihe* | *it's my turn* |
| **rein** → schmutzig | pure; clean; neat |
| *ins reine schreiben* | *to make a fair copy (of)* |
| *reinen Tisch machen* | *to make a clean sweep* |
| *reinigen* | *to clean* |
| *die Reinigung* | *cleaning* |
| **die 'Reise** /n | voyage; journey; travel |
| *gute Reise!* | *a pleasant journey!* |
| *eine Reise machen* | *to go on a journey, to take a trip* |
| *das Reisegepäck* | *luggage* |
| **'reisen** | to travel |
| *ins Ausland reisen* | *to go abroad* |
| *von . . . nach . . . über . . . reisen* | *to go from . . . to . . . via . . .* |
| *der Reisende* | *traveller, passenger* |
| **'reißen** i-i | to tear; to tear off |
| *in Stücke reißen* | *to tear to pieces* |
| *ein Loch reißen* | *to tear a hole* |
| *der Faden reißt* | *the thread breaks* |
| **'reiten** i-i | to ride; to be/go on horseback |
| **die Religi'on** /en | religion |
| *religiös* | *religious* |
| **'rennen** a-a | to run |

| | |
|---|---|
| **die Repara'tur** /en | repair(s) |
| *in Reparatur* | *under repair* |
| *in Reparatur geben* | *to have repaired* |
| *die Reparaturwerkstatt* | *service station, repair shop* |
| *reparieren* | *to repair* |
| *reparieren lassen* | *to have repaired* |
| **die Repu'blik** /en | republic |
| **der Rest** es/e | rest |
| **das Restau'rant** s/s (cf. Gasthaus) | restaurant |
| **'retten** | to save |
| **die Revoluti'on** /en | revolution |
| **richten** | to direct |
| *sich richten (an)* | *to address o.s.* (*to*) |
| **der 'Richter** s/- | judge |
| **'richtig** → falsch | right, exact, correct |
| *richtig!* | *right! quite* (*so*)*!* |
| *richtig rechnen* | *to calculate correctly* |
| *die Uhr geht richtig* | *the watch/clock is right* |
| **die 'Richtung** /en | direction, way |
| *in dieser Richtung* | *this way* |
| *in Richtung auf* | *in the direction of* |
| *in der entgegengesetzten Richtung* | *in the opposite direction* |
| **'riechen** o-o **(nach)** | to smell (of) |
| *gut / schlecht riechen* | *to smell good/bad* |
| *riechen (an)* | *to take a sniff* (*at*) |
| **rief** (1st, 3rd pers sg pret of **rufen**) | |
| **das Rind** s/er | cattle |
| *das Rindfleisch* | *beef* |
| **der Ring** s/e | ring; circle; link |
| *einen Ring tragen* | *to wear a ring* |
| **rings**(um(her)) | around, round about |
| **der Rock** s/ö-e | coat; skirt |
| **roh** | raw; coarse, rough |
| **die 'Rolle** /n | roll(er); part, role |

| | |
|---|---|
| *rollen* | *to roll* |
| **der Ro'man** s/e | novel |
| **die 'Rose** /n | rose |
| **rot** / röter / am rötesten | red |
| *rot werden* | *to turn red* |
| *das Rote Kreuz* | *the Red Cross* |
| *bei Rot halten* | *to stop at the red light* |
| **der 'Rücken** s/- | back |
| *die Rückseite* | *back* |
| **die 'Rückkehr** | return |
| *bie meiner Rückkehr* | *on my return* |
| *(die) Rückfahrkarte* | *return (ticket)* |
| **'rückwärts** → vorwärts | backward(s) |
| *rückwärtsfahren* | *to back* |
| **der Ruf** s/e | call, cry |
| *die Rufnummer* | *(tele)phone number* |
| **'rufen** ie-u | to call, to cry |
| *(um) Hilfe rufen* | *to call for help* |
| *die Polizei rufen* | *to call for the police* |
| **die 'Ruhe** | rest, calm, silence |
| *Ruhe!* | *silence! be quiet!* |
| *laß mich in Ruhe!* | *leave me alone!* |
| *nur die Ruhe!* | *easy does it! take it easy!* |
| *die Ruhe bewahren* | *to keep calm* |
| **'ruhen** | to rest |
| **'ruhig** → unruhig | calm, quiet |
| *sei ruhig!* | *keep quiet!* |
| *ruhig bleiben* | *to keep calm* |
| *ruhig schlafen* | *to sleep peacefully* |
| **der Ruhm** s | glory, fame |
| **(sich) 'rühren** | to stir/move; to touch |
| *rühren Sie sich nicht!* | *don't stir!* |
| *das rührt ihn nicht* | *that doesn't touch him* |
| **rund** | round |
| **der 'Rundfunk** s | wireless, radio, sound |
| *im Rundfunk* | *on the wireless/radio* |
| **'runter** (cf. herunter) | |

## S

| | |
|---|---|
| **die 'Sache** /n | thing; affair, matter |
| *das ist meine Sache* | *that's my affair* |
| *das ist Ihre Sache* | *that's your business* |
| *eine Sache für sich* | *a separate matter* |
| *das ist eine andere Sache* | *that's another matter* |
| *das ist nicht deine Sache* | *that's no business of yours* |
| *zur Sache!* | *(back) to the subject!* |
| *so steht die Sache* | *that's how matters stand* |
| *das gehört nicht zur Sache* | *that's beside the point* |
| *die Sache ist erledigt* | *that settles the matter* |
| **der Sack** s/ä-e | sack, bag |
| **'säen** | to sow |
| **der Saft** s/ä-e | juice |
| **'sagen** | to say, to tell |
| *sag! was du nicht sagst!* | *you don't say (so)!* |
| *man sagt* | *they say* |
| *Dank sagen (für)* | *to thank (for)* |
| *das hat nichts zu sagen* | *it does not matter* |
| *wie sagt man . . . auf deutsch?* | *what is the German for . . .?* |
| *das sagt man nicht* | *that's not the proper thing to say* |
| *was wollen Sie damit sagen?* | *what do you mean by that?* |
| **sah** (1st, 3rd pers sg pret of **sehen**) | |
| **das Salz** es/e | salt |
| *ist Salz daran?* | *is it salted?* |
| *die Speisen salzen* | *to salt the dishes* |
| *salzig* | *salty* |
| **'sammeln** | to gather, to collect |
| *Briefmarken sammeln* | *to collect stamps* |
| *die Sammlung* | *collection* |
| **'sämtliche** | all (together) |
| *sämtliche Werke* pl | *complete works* |
| **der Sand** s/e | sand |

| | |
|---|---|
| **sanft** → heftig | gentle |
| **saß** (1st, 3rd pers sg pret of **sitzen**) | sat |
| **satt sein** → hungrig sein | to have had enough |
| *sich satt essen* | *to eat o's fill* |
| *ich habe es satt* | *I'm sick of it* |
| **der Satz** es/ä-e | sentence; leap, bound |
| *einen Satz machen* | *to take a leap* |
| *in einem Satz* | *with one bound/leap* |
| *ein Satz Briefmarken* | *a set of stamps* |
| **'sauber** → schmutzig | clean |
| *sauber machen* | *to clean (up)* |
| *ein sauberes Heft* | *a clean exercise-book* |
| **'sauer** → süß | sour; acid |
| *sauer werden* | *to turn sour* |
| *die Milch ist sauer* | *the milk has turned (sour)* |
| *es wird ihm sauer* | *he's finding it tough (going)* |
| **die 'Schachtel** /n | box, case |
| *eine Schachtel Streichhölzer* | *a box of matches* |
| *eine Schachtel Zigaretten* | *a packet of cigarettes* |
| es ist **'schade** | it's a pity |
| *wie schade!* | *what a pity!* |
| **'schaden** → nützen | to do harm, to hurt |
| *das schadet nichts* | *that does not matter* |
| **der 'Schaden** s/ä → Nutzen | harm, damage |
| *Schaden anrichten* | *to do harm, to cause damage* |
| *Schaden erleiden* | *to suffer harm* |
| *Schaden wieder gutmachen* | *to repair the damage* |
| **das Schaf** s/e | sheep |
| **'schaffen** / erschaffen u-a | to create |
| *er hat ein Meisterwerk geschaffen* | *he has created a masterpiece* |
| **'schaffen** | to work; to do |
| *er schafft den ganzen Tag* | *he is busy all day long* |

| | |
|---|---|
| *ich habe es geschafft* | *I managed it* |
| *nach Hause schaffen* | *to take home* |
| *zur Post schaffen* | *to post* |
| *ins Krankenhaus schaffen* | *to take to the hospital* |
| **'schälen** | to peel |
| *Kartoffeln schälen* | *to peel potatoes* |
| **die 'Schallplatte** /n | record |
| *eine Schallplatte / Platte auflegen* | *to put on a record* |
| **'schalten** (rauf / runter) | to change gear, to change up/down |
| *der Schalter* | *switch, knob* |
| **scharf** | sharp, keen |
| *scharf einstellen* | *to bring into focus* |
| **der 'Schatten** s/- → Licht | shade; shadow |
| *im Schatten* | *in the shade* |
| *in den Schatten stellen* | *to put in the shade* |
| *Schatten werfen (auf)* | *to cast a shadow (upon)* |
| **'schätzen** | to estimate; to value |
| *sich glücklich schätzen* | *to be happy (to)* |
| *wie alt schätzt du ihn?* | *how old do you think he is?* |
| **das 'Schauspiel** s/e | spectacle; play |
| **der Scheck** s/s | cheque |
| **der Schein** s/e | shine, light; note, ***am*** bill |
| *bei / im Sonnenschein* | *in the sun(shine)* |
| *zwei Zehnmarkscheine* | *two 10-mark notes* |
| *den Schein wahren* | *to keep up appearances* |
| **'scheinen** ie-ie | to shine; to seem, to appear |
| *der Mond scheint* | *the moon is shining* |
| *es scheint* | *it seems* |
| *mir scheint* | *it seems to me* |
| *er scheint krank zu sein* | *he appears to be ill* |
| **der 'Scheinwerfer** /s- | headlight |
| **'schenken** | to give, to present |
| *jdm etwas schenken* | *to give s.o. a present* |

| | |
|---|---|
| **die 'Schere** /n | scissors |
| *eine Schere* | *a pair of scissors* |
| **'schicken** | to send |
| *mit der Post schicken* | *to (send by) post* |
| *ins Haus schicken* | *to deliver (to)* |
| *nach dem Arzt schicken* | *to send for the doctor* |
| **das 'Schicksal** s/e | destiny, fortune, fate |
| **'schieben** o-o → ziehen | to push |
| *den Wagen schieben* | *to push the car* |
| **schief** → gerade | inclined, leaning, sloping, tilted |
| **schien** (1st, 3rd pers sg pret of **scheinen**) | |
| **'schießen** o-o **(auf)** | to shoot (at) |
| *schieß los!* | *fire away!* |
| *ein Tor schießen* | *to score a goal* |
| *eine Rakete abschießen* | *to launch a rocket* |
| **das Schiff** s/e | ship, boat |
| *mit dem Schiff fahren* | *to travel by ship* |
| *auf dem Schiff* | *on board (the ship)* |
| **der Schirm** s/e | screen |
| *der (Regen)schirm* | *umbrella* |
| **die Schlacht** /en | battle |
| **der Schlaf** s | sleep |
| *im Schlaf* | *in o's sleep* |
| *ein Schläfchen machen* | *to take a nap* |
| *das Schlafzimmer* | *bedroom* |
| **'schlafen** ie-a/ä → wachen | to sleep, to be asleep |
| *schlafen gehen* | *to go to sleep/to bed* |
| *schlafen Sie gut!* | *sleep well* |
| *fest schlafen* | *to sleep soundly* |
| *einschlafen* | *to fall asleep* |
| *eingeschlafen sein* | *to have fallen asleep* |
| **der Schlag** s/ä-e | blow, knock |
| *einen Schlag versetzen* | *to strike a blow* |
| *Schlag auf Schlag* | *blow upon blow* |
| *auf einen Schlag* | *at one blow* |
| *Schlag 5 (Uhr)* | *on the stroke of 5* |

| | |
|---|---|
| **'schlagen** u-a/ä | to strike, to beat, to knock |
| *mit dem Stock schlagen* | *to beat with a stick* |
| *das Herz schlägt mir* | *my heart beats* |
| *es schlägt zehn (Uhr)* | *it's striking ten* (*o'clock*) |
| *einen Nagel in die Wand schlagen* | *to drive a nail into the wall* |
| **schlecht** → gut | bad |
| *nicht schlecht* | *not* (*at all*) *bad* |
| *mir ist schlecht* | *I feel ill/sick* |
| *es geht mir schlecht* | *I'm in a bad way* |
| *immer schlechter* | *worse and worse* |
| *schlecht aussehen* | *to look ill* |
| *es ist schlechtes Wetter* | *the weather is bad* |
| **'schließen** o-o → öffnen | to shut, to close |
| *in die Arme schließen* | *to embrace* |
| *einen Vertrag schließen* | *to conclude a treaty, enter into a contract* |
| *den Brief schließen* | *to finish the letter* |
| **'schließlich** | finally, at length, after all |
| *schließlich etwas tun* | *to end by doing sth.* |
| **schlimm** → gut | bad; evil |
| *umso schlimmer* | *all the worse, so much the worse* |
| *das ist nicht so schlimm* | *it's not as bad as all that* |
| *ein schlimmes Ende nehmen* | *to come to a bad end* |
| *schlimmstenfalls* | *at the worst* |
| *nichts Schlimmes* | *nothing serious* |
| das **Schloß** sses/össer | lock; castle |
| der **Schluck** s/e | mouthful |
| *einen Schluck nehmen* | *to have a sip* |
| *schlucken* | *to swallow* |
| der **Schluß** sses/üsse → Anfang | close; end |
| *Schluß machen (mit)* | *to put an end* (*to*), *to finish* (*with*) |

| | |
|---|---|
| *Schluß!* | *done! finished!* |
| *Schluß damit!* | *stop it! that will do!* |
| der **'Schlüssel** s/- | key |
| *der Schlüssel steckt* | *the key is in the lock* |
| *den Schlüssel stecken lassen* | *to leave the key in the lock* |
| **schmal** / schmäler / am schmälsten → breit | narrow |
| **'schmecken** | to taste |
| *gut schmecken* | *to taste good* |
| *bitter schmecken* | *to have a bitter taste* |
| *(wie) schmeckt's?* | *do you like it?* |
| der **Schmerz** es/en | pain, ache |
| *heftige Schmerzen* | *severe pains* |
| *ich habe Schmerzen* | *I feel pains* |
| *Kopfschmerzen haben* | *to have a headache* |
| *schmerzen* | *to be painful* |
| *es schmerzt mich* | *it gives me pain* |
| *schmerzhaft* | *painful* |
| **'schmutzig** → sauber, rein | dirty |
| *schmutzig machen* | *to dirty* |
| der **Schnee** s | snow |
| **'schneiden** i-i | to cut |
| *in Stücke schneiden* | *to cut up* |
| *sich die Haare schneiden lassen* | *to have o's hair cut* |
| *sich in den Finger schneiden* | *to cut o's finger* |
| *der Schneider* | *tailor, dressmaker* |
| **schnell** → langsam | quick, rapid, swift; fast |
| *schnell!* | *be quick! hurry up!* |
| *so schnell wie möglich* | *as quickly as possible* |
| *machen Sie schnell!* | *hurry up!* |
| *schnell fahren* | *to drive fast* |
| der **'Schnupfen** s | cold |
| die **Schnur** /ü-e | cord, string |
| die **Schoko'lade** /n | chocolate |
| *eine Tafel Schokolade* | *a bar of chocolate* |

| | |
|---|---|
| **schon**/bereits | already |
| *schon jetzt* | *already* |
| *schon lange* | *for a long time* |
| *heute schon* | *this very day* |
| *er wird schon kommen* | *he is sure to come* |
| **schön** → häßlich | beautiful, fine |
| *wie schön!* | *how nice/beautiful!* |
| *es war so schön!* | *it was (so) beautiful/ wonderful!* |
| *es ist heute schön (es Wetter)* | *the weather is fine today* |
| *danke schön!* | *many thanks* |
| *bitte schön!* | *don't mention it* |
| **die 'Schönheit** /en | beauty |
| **der Schrank** s/ä-e | wardrobe; cupboard |
| **der 'Schreck(en)** s/- | fright; terror, horror |
| *schrecklich* | *frightful; terrible* |
| **'schreiben** ie-ie | to write |
| *ins reine schreiben* | *to write out a fair copy* |
| *mit der Maschine schreiben* | *to type* |
| *die Schreibmaschine* | *typewriter* |
| **'schreien** ie-ie | to cry, to shout |
| *vor Schmerz schreien* | *to cry with pain* |
| **'schreiten** i-i | to walk |
| **die Schrift** /en | writing |
| *das Schriftstück* | *document* |
| *der Schriftsteller* | *writer* |
| *schriftlich* | *written* |
| **der Schritt** s/e | step |
| *Schritt für Schritt* | *step by step* |
| *auf Schritt und Tritt* | *at every step/turn* |
| *mit schnellen Schritten* | *at a brisk pace* |
| *Schritte unternehmen* | *to take steps* |
| *Schritt halten (mit)* | *to keep step (with)* |
| *Schritt fahren!* | *Drive slowly* |
| **der Schuh** s/e | shoe, boot |
| *ein Paar Schuhe* | *a pair of shoes* |

| | |
|---|---|
| *die Schuhe putzen* | *to polish o's shoes* |
| *die Schuhe anziehen / ausziehen* | *to put on/take off o's shoes* |
| **die Schuld** /en | fault; debt |
| *es ist meine Schuld* | *it is my fault* |
| *wer ist schuld?* | *whose fault is it?* |
| *schuld sein (an)* | *to be to blame (for)* |
| *Schulden machen* | *to run into debt* |
| *seine Schulden bezahlen* | *to pay o's debts* |
| *schieb die Schuld nicht auf mich* | *don't put the blame on me* |
| **'schulden** | to owe |
| **'schuldig** | guilty |
| *was bin ich schuldig?* | *how much do I owe you?* |
| **die Schule** /n | school |
| *in der Schule* | *at school* |
| *in die Schule gehen* | *to go to school* |
| *Schule haben* | *to have lessons* |
| *eine Schule besuchen* | *to go to a school* |
| *Schularbeiten machen* | *to do o's homework* |
| **der 'Schüler** s/- | pupil, schoolboy |
| **die 'Schulter** /n | shoulder |
| **der Schuß** sses/üsse | shot |
| **die 'Schüssel** /n | dish, bowl |
| **'schütteln** | to shake |
| *die Hand schütteln* | *to shake hands (with)* |
| *vor Gebrauch schütteln* | *shake well before use* |
| **der Schutz** es | protection |
| *in Schutz nehmen* | *to defend* |
| *Schutz suchen* | *to take shelter* |
| **'schützen (vor)** | *to protect (from)* |
| *geschützt (gegen)* | *safe (from), protected (against)* |
| **schwach** → stark | weak |
| *mir wird schwach* | *I am feeling faint* |
| *eine Schwäche haben (für)* | *to have a weakness (for)* |

| | |
|---|---|
| **der Schwamm** s/ä-e | sponge |
| *mit dem Schwamm wegwischen* | *to sponge out* |
| **der Schwanz** es/ä-e | tail |
| *der Hund wedelt mit dem Schwanz* | *the dog wags its tail* |
| **schwarz** | black |
| *ins Schwarze treffen* | *to hit the nail on the head* |
| *schwarz auf weiß* | *in black and white* |
| **'schweigen** ie-ie → reden | to be silent |
| *ganz zu schweigen von* | *to say nothing of* |
| *schweigend* | *in silence* |
| **das Schwein** s/e | pig |
| **schwer** → leicht | heavy; difficult; serious |
| *5 Pfund schwer sein* | *to weigh 5 pounds* |
| *schwer arbeiten* | *to work hard* |
| *eine schwere Arbeit* | *hard work* |
| *ein schwerer Fehler* | *a bad mistake* |
| *schwer krank* | *seriously ill* |
| *schwer verletzt* | *seriously injured* |
| **die 'Schwester** /n | sister |
| **'schwierig** → leicht | difficult |
| *ein schwieriger Punkt* | *a knotty problem* |
| **die 'Schwierigkeit** /en | difficulty |
| *ohne Schwierigkeit* | *without difficulty* |
| *in Schwierigkeiten sein* | *to be in trouble* |
| *in Schwierigkeiten geraten* | *to get into difficulties* |
| **'schwimmen** a-o | to swim, to take a swim |
| *schwimmen gehen* | *to go for a swim* |
| *durch einen Fluß schwimmen* | *to swim across a river* |
| *gegen den Strom schwimmen* | *to swim against the current* |
| **'schwitzen** | to sweat, to perspire |
| **der See** s/n | lake |
| **die See** /n | sea |
| *auf See* | *at sea* |

| | |
|---|---|
| *an die See fahren* | *to go to the seaside* |
| *an der See* | *by the sea(side)* |
| *zur See gehen* | *to go to sea* |
| *seekrank sein* | *to be seasick* |
| **die 'Seele** /n | soul |
| *mit Leib und Seele dabei sein* | *to put o's heart and soul into sth.* |
| **das 'Segel** s/- | sail |
| *mit vollen Segeln* | *under full sail* |
| **'sehen** a-e/ie | to see; to look |
| *sieh mal an!* | *I say!* |
| *sieh mich an!* | *look at me* |
| *sieh dich um!* | *look around you* |
| *sieh nach rechts!* | *look right* |
| *laß mal sehen!* | *let me see* |
| *gut sehen* | *to have good eyesight* |
| *schlecht sehen* | *to have bad eyesight* |
| *klar sehen* | *to see clearly* |
| *mit eignen Augen sehen* | *to see with o's own eyes* |
| *sieh nach der Uhr, wie spät es ist* | *see what time it is by your watch* |
| *vom Sehen kennen* | *to know by sight* |
| *im Fernsehen sehen* | *to see on television* |
| *fernsehen* | *to watch television* |
| *der Fernsehzuschauer* | *(tele)viewer* |
| **sehr** → wenig | very; much |
| *sehr gern* | *(most) willingly* |
| *sehr gut* | *very good/well* |
| *sehr viele* | *a great many* |
| *das gefällt mir sehr* | *I like it very much* |
| *danke sehr!* | *thanks very much* |
| *bitte sehr!* | *don't mention it* |
| **sei** (imp of **sein**) | be |
| **die 'Seife** /n | soap |
| *ein Stück Seife* | *a cake of soap* |
| **sein,** war—gewesen | to be; to exist |
| *wer ist da?* | *who's there?* |
| *ich bin's* | *it's me* |

| | |
|---|---|
| *bist du's?* | *is it you?* |
| *da bin ich* | *here I am* |
| *was ist das?* | *what's that?* |
| *was soll das sein?* | *what does that mean?* |
| *laß das sein!* | *stop that!* |
| **'seinetwegen** | because of him |
| **seit** | since |
| *seit wann?* | *since when?* |
| *seit gestern* | *since yesterday* |
| *seit langem* | *for a long time* |
| *seit 3 Jahren* | (*for*) *3 years* |
| **seit'dem** | (ever) since |
| **die 'Seite** /n | side; page |
| *auf der rechten Seite* | *on the right*(*-hand side*) |
| *an meiner Seite* | *by my side* |
| *auf seiner Seite* | *on his side* |
| *geh zur Seite!* | *step aside* |
| *auf beiden Seiten* | *on both sides* |
| *von allen Seiten* | *from all sides* |
| *nach allen Seiten* | *in all directions* |
| *Seite an Seite* | *side by side* |
| *das ist nicht seine starke Seite* | *that's not his strong point* |
| *wir sind auf Seite 3* | *we are on page 3* |
| **die Se'kunde** /n | second |
| **'selber / selbst** | self; even |
| *ich selbst* | *I myself* |
| *selbst seine Freunde* | *even his friends* |
| *das versteht sich von selbst* | *that goes without saying* |
| **'selbstverständlich** | (as a matter) of course |
| *aber selbstverständlich!* | *why, certainly! naturally!* |
| *es ist selbstverstandlich, daß* | *it goes without saying that* |
| **'selten** → oft / häufig | rarely, seldom |
| *nicht selten* | *pretty often* |
| *ein seltener Vogel* | *a rare bird* |

| | |
|---|---|
| **'senden** (a-a) → empfangen | to send; to broadcast |
| *Bitte nachsenden!* | *Please forward* |
| *ein Programm senden* | *to broadcast/telecast a a programme* |
| **der 'Sessel** s/- | armchair |
| **'setzen** | to put; to place |
| *alles daran setzen* | *to do o's utmost* |
| *in Gang setzen* | *to set going* |
| *sich setzen* | *to sit down, to take a seat* |
| *setzen Sie sich!* | *sit down, take a seat* |
| *sich zu Tisch setzen* | *to sit down at table* |
| *sich in den Wagen setzen* | *to get into the car* |
| **sich** | oneself; each other |
| *sie lieben sich* | *they love each other* |
| **'sicher** → unsicher | sure; certain |
| *sicher (vor)* | *safe (from)* |
| *es wird sicher regnen* | *it's sure to rain* |
| *sicher!* | *certainly!* |
| *sicher nicht* | *certainly not* |
| **die 'Sicherheit** /en | safety |
| *in Sicherheit bringen* | *to put in a safe place* |
| *die Sicherheitsnadel* | *safety-pin* |
| **'sichtbar** → unsichtbar | visible |
| **der Sieg** s/e | victory |
| **sieht** (3rd pers sg pres of **sehen**) | sees |
| **das 'Silber** s | silver |
| *aus Silber* | *made of silver* |
| **sind** (1st, 3rd pers pl pres of **sein**) | are |
| **'singen** a-u | to sing |
| *ein Lied singen* | *to sing a song* |
| *falsch singen* | *to sing out of tune* |
| **'sinken** a-u → steigen | to sink |
| *den Mut sinken lassen* | *to lose courage* |
| *die Preise sinken* | *(the) prices are going down* |

| | |
|---|---|
| **der Sinn** s/(e) | sense; meaning |
| *die 5 Sinne* | *the five senses* |
| *das hat keinen Sinn* | *that doesn't make sense, there is no point in that* |
| *ganz in meinem Sinne* | *just to my liking* |
| *im wahrsten Sinne des Wortes* | *in the truest sense of the word* |
| *im Sinn haben* | *to have in mind* |
| **'sittlich** → unsittlich | moral |
| **der Sitz** es/e | seat |
| **'sitzen** a-e | to sit |
| *bleiben Sie sitzen!* | *keep your seat(s), don't get up* |
| *bei Tisch sitzen* | *to sit at (the) table* |
| *dieser Anzug sitzt gut* | *this suit fits well* |
| **die 'Sitzung** /en | session, meeting |
| **so** | so; thus; that way; like this/that |
| *so!* | *that's that!; there!* |
| *so?* | *indeed?* |
| *so, so!* | *well, well!* |
| *ach so!* | *oh, I see!* |
| *so ist es* | *that's how it is* |
| *und nicht so* | *and not like that* |
| *und so weiter* | *and so on* |
| *so siehst du aus!* | *you don't say; that's just like you* |
| *so groß wie* | *as big as* |
| *nicht so groß wie* | *not so big as* |
| **die 'Socke** /n | sock |
| **so'eben** / eben | just (now) |
| *soeben erschienen* | *just published* |
| **das 'Sofa** s/s | sofa |
| **so'fort** → später | at once; directly |
| **so'gar** | even; yet |
| **soge'nannt** | so-called; would-be, pretended |

| | |
|---|---|
| **der Sohn** s/ö-e | son |
| **so'lange** | while, as long as |
| **'solche(r,s)** | such |
| *ein solcher Mensch, solch ein Mensch* | *such a man* |
| *solche Menschen* pl | *such people* |
| **der Sol'dat** en/en | soldier |
| **'sollen** | to be to; to have to |
| *ich soll morgen fahren* | *I am to/should go tomorrow* |
| *was (soll ich) tun?* | *what am I to do?* |
| *sag ihm, er soll kommen* | *tell him to come* |
| *sollten Sie ihn sehen* | *if you should see him* |
| *man sollte meinen* | *one would think* |
| *ich sollte eigentlich arbeiten* | *I ought to work* |
| *er soll krank sein* | *he is supposed to be ill* |
| **der 'Sommer** s/- | summer |
| *im Sommer* | *in summer* |
| *der Sommer ist vorbei* | *summer is over* |
| **'sonderbar** | singular, strange |
| **'sondern** (im Gegenteil) | but (on the contrary) |
| *nicht nur . . . , sondern auch* | *not only . . . , but also* |
| **die 'Sonne** /n | sun |
| *in der Sonne* | *in the sun* |
| *ein Platz an der Sonne* | *a place in the sun* |
| *die Sonne scheint* | *the sun is shining* |
| *die aufgehende / untergehende Sonne* | *the rising/setting sun* |
| *die Sonne geht auf* | *the sun is rising* |
| *die Sonne geht unter* | *the sun is setting* |
| *im Sonnenschein* | *in the sun shine* |
| **sonst** | otherwise, or else; as a rule |
| *was sonst noch?* | *what else? anything else?* |
| *sonst nichts* | *nothing else* |
| *wie sonst* | *as usual* |

| | |
|---|---|
| *was gibt es sonst Neues?* | *any other news?* |
| die 'Sorge /n | care; sorrow, worry, trouble |
| *sich Sorgen machen (um)* | *to be worried (about)* |
| *machen Sie sich keine Sorgen!* | *don't worry* |
| *laß das meine Sorge sein!* | *leave that to me* |
| 'sorgen | to care (for), to look (after), to see (to) |
| *dafür sorge ich* | *I'll see to that* |
| *er sorgt für die Familie* | *he takes care of the family* |
| *sich sorgen (um)* | *to be uneasy, to worry (about)* |
| 'sorgfältig | with care; carefully |
| so'viel → sowenig | as far as |
| *doppelt soviel* | *twice as much* |
| *soviel ich weiß* | *as far as I know* |
| *soviel wie möglich* | *as much/often as possible* |
| *so viel / so viele* | *so much/so many* |
| so'wie | as well as |
| sowie'so | in any case, anyhow/ anyway, as it is |
| die So'wjetunion, die UdSSR | the Soviet Union, the U.S.S.R. |
| so'wohl . . . als auch | as well as |
| sozi'al | social |
| sozu'sagen | so to speak |
| 'spalten → vereinen | to split; to divide |
| 'spannen → lösen | to stretch; to tighten |
| *spannend* | *exciting; thrilling* |
| *gespannt sein (auf)* | *to be curious (about)* |
| *die Spannung* | *tension; close attention* |
| 'sparen | to save (up)/put by; to spare |
| der Spaß es/ä-e → Ernst | fun; joke |
| *aus / zum Spaß* | *for (the) fun (of it)* |
| *viel Spaß!* | *have a good time* |

| | |
|---|---|
| *Spaß beiseite!* | *joking apart* |
| *es macht mir Spaß* | *I like it (a lot)* |
| *er versteht keinen Spaß* | *he cannot see a joke* |
| *spaßig* | *funny* |
| **spät** → früh / zeitig | late |
| *es ist spät* | *it is late* |
| *es wird spät* | *it's getting late* |
| *wie spät ist es?* | *what's the time?* |
| *zu spät* | *too late* |
| *(5 Minuten) zu spät kommen* | *to be (five minutes) late* |
| *spät nachts* | *late at night* |
| **'später** | later (on) |
| *früher oder später* | *sooner or later* |
| **spa'zierenfahren** u-a/ä | to go for a drive |
| **spazierengehen** i-a | to go for a walk |
| *der Spaziergang* | *walk* |
| *einen Spaziergang machen* | *to go for a walk* |
| **die 'Speise** /n | food; dish |
| *die Speisekarte* | *menu* |
| **der 'Spiegel** s/- | mirror, (looking-) glass |
| *sieh in den Spiegel* | *look (at yourself) in the mirror* |
| **das Spiel** s/e | play; game; match |
| *wie steht das Spiel?* | *what's the score?* |
| *der Spielplatz* | *playground, playing field* |
| **'spielen** | to play |
| *ein Spiel spielen* | *to play a game* |
| *Karten spielen* | *to play cards* |
| *ein Instrument spielen* | *to play an instrument* |
| *Geige spielen* | *to play the violin* |
| *eine Rolle spielen* | *to play/act a part* |
| *einen Film spielen* | *to show a film* |
| **spitz** | pointed; sharp |
| **die 'Spitze** /n | point; head |
| *an der Spitze* | *in the lead; ahead* |

| | |
|---|---|
| *an der Spitze stehen* | *to be at the head (of)* |
| *wer ist an der Spitze?* | *who's at the head/in the lead?* |
| *den Bleistift spitzen* | *to sharpen the pencil* |
| **der Sport** s/Sportarten | sport |
| *Sport treiben* | *to go in for sport* |
| *der Sportler* | *sportsman* |
| **sprach** (1st, 3rd pers sg pret of **sprechen**) | |
| **die 'Sprache** /n | language; speech |
| *fremde Sprachen* | *foreign languages* |
| *lebende Sprachen* | *living languages* |
| *eine Sprache lernen* | *to learn a language* |
| *eine Sprache sprechen* | *to speak a language* |
| *er kann mehrere Sprachen* | *he speaks several languages* |
| **'sprechen** a-o/i → schweigen | to speak |
| *deutsch sprechen* | *to speak German* |
| *laut sprechen* | *to speak loudly/in a loud voice* |
| *sprich lauter!* | *speak up* |
| *leise sprechen* | *to speak quietly/in a low voice* |
| *kein Wort sprechen* | *not to open o's mouth* |
| *ist Herr X zu sprechen?* | *may I see Mr X?* |
| *er wünscht Sie zu sprechen* | *he wishes to see you* |
| *wir sprechen deutsch* | *German spoken* |
| *bitte hier sprechen* | *speak here* |
| *hier spricht . . .* | *this is . . . speaking* |
| **'springen** a-u | to spring; to jump |
| *über einen Graben springen* | *to jump a ditch* |
| *ins Wasser springen* | *to jump into the water* |
| *aus dem Bett springen* | *to jump out of bed* |
| *in Stücke springen* | *to fall to pieces* |
| *die Scheibe ist gesprungen* | *the pane is cracked* |

| | |
|---|---|
| *vor Freude springen* | *to jump for joy* |
| *in die Augen springen* | *to strike the eye* |
| **die Spur** /en | trace |
| *keine Spur!* | *not a bit! not at all!* |
| *keine Spur von . . .* | *not a trace of . . .* |
| *auf die Spur kommen* | *to get on* (s.o.'s) *track* |
| **der Staat** s/en | state |
| *die Staatsangehörigkeit* | *nationality* |
| *der Staatsmann* | *statesman* |
| *das Staatsoberhaupt* | *the head of state* |
| **der Stab** s/ä-e | staff, stick |
| **die Stadt** /ä-e | town, city |
| *die ganze Stadt* | *the whole town* |
| *in der Stadt* | *in town* |
| *in die Stadt gehen* | *to go to town* |
| *(die) Stadtmitte* | *town centre* |
| *eine Stadtrundfahrt* | *a tour of the town* |
| **der Stahl** s/ä-e | steel |
| *aus Stahl* | *made of steel* |
| **der Stall** s/ä-e | stable; cow-shed |
| **der Stamm** s/ä-e | trunk, stem; parent stock; tribe |
| **stand** (1st, 3rd pers sg pret of **stehen**) | stood |
| **der Stand** es/ä-e | position; profession |
| *gut im Stande sein* | *to be in good condition* |
| *imstande / außerstande sein (zu)* | *to be able/unable* (*to*) |
| **der 'Standpunkt** es/e | point of view |
| *auf dem Standpunkt stehen, daß* | *to take the view that* |
| **stark** / stärker / am stärksten → schwach | strong; great; powerful |
| *das ist ein starkes Stück!* | *that's a bit thick!* |
| *eine starke Erkältung* | *a bad cold* |
| **die 'Stärke** /n → Schwäche | strength; force; power |
| *seine Stärke* | *his strong point* |

| | |
|---|---|
| **der Start** s/e,s → Ziel / Landung | start; take-off |
| *Start und Ziel* | *start and finish* |
| *Start frei!* | *Clear for take-off* |
| **'starten** → ankommen / landen | to start; to take off |
| **'statt\|finden** a-u | to take place |
| **der Staub** s | dust; powder |
| *Staub wischen* | *to dust* |
| *der Staublappen* | *duster* |
| *der Staubsauger* | *vacuum cleaner* |
| **'staunen (über)** | to be astonished (at) |
| **'stechen** a-o/i | to sting, to prick |
| **'stehen** a-a | to stand |
| *die Uhr steht* | *the watch/clock has stopped* |
| *wie steht's?* | *how do you do? how are you?* |
| *wie steht das Spiel?* | *what's the score?* |
| *wie die Dinge stehen* | *as things stand* |
| *offen stehen* | *to be open* |
| *das steht Ihnen gut* | *it becomes you* |
| *wie steht es um . . .?* | *what about . . .?* |
| *stehenbleiben* | *to stop* |
| *nicht stehenbleiben!* | *move on! keep moving!* |
| **'stehend** | standing |
| **'stehlen** a-o/ie | to steal |
| **'steigen** ie-ie, **hi'nauf\|steigen** → fallen / sinken | to climb, to go up, to ascend |
| *herab-/hinabsteigen* | *to climb/go down, to descend* |
| *auf den Berg steigen* | *to climb a mountain* |
| *in den Wagen steigen* | *to get into the car* |
| *aufs Rad steigen* | *to mount the bicycle* |
| *aus dem Wagen steigen* | *to get out of the car* |
| *die Preise steigen* | *prices are rising* |
| **der Stein s/e** | stone |

| | |
|---|---|
| *aus Stein* | *made of stone* |
| *einen Stein werfen (auf)* | *to throw a stone (at)* |
| *die Steinkohle* | *hard coal* |
| **die 'Stelle** /n | place, spot; post |
| *auf der Stelle* | *on the spot, this minute, then and there* |
| *an Stelle von* | *in place of* |
| *von einer Stelle zur andern* | *from one place to another* |
| *ich an Ihrer Stelle* | *if I were you* |
| *eine Stelle erhalten* | *to get a post/job* |
| *eine Stelle suchen* | *to look for a post* |
| *zur Stelle sein* | *to be present* |
| *an erster Stelle* | *in the first place* |
| *an Ort und Stelle* | *on the spot* |
| **'stellen** | to put; to place; to set |
| *auf den Tisch stellen* | *to put on the table* |
| *in die Ecke stellen* | *to put in the corner* |
| *die Uhr stellen* | *to set the watch/clock* |
| *leiser stellen* | *to turn lower* |
| *anstellen* | *to turn on; to take on, employ* |
| *abstellen* | *to turn off* |
| *eine Aufgabe stellen* | *to set a task* |
| *eine Frage stellen* | *to ask a question* |
| *in Frage stellen* | *to call into question, to doubt* |
| *sich dumm stellen* | *to play the fool* |
| **die 'Stellung** /en | position; situation; condition, standing |
| *eine Stellung suchen* | *to look for a job* |
| **'sterben** a-o/i | to die; to pass away |
| **der Stern** s/e | star |
| *unter einem guten Stern* | *under a lucky star* |
| **stets** | always |
| **still** → laut | still; calm; silent |
| *(sei) still!* | *(be) quiet! silence!* |
| *im stillen* | *secretly* |

| | |
|---|---|
| *stillstehen* | *to stand still* |
| die **'Stille** | silence |
| die **'Stimme** /n | voice |
| *mit lauter Stimme* | *in a loud voice* |
| *mit leiser Stimme* | *in a low voice* |
| *seine Stimme erheben* | *to raise o's voice* |
| *seine Stimme abgeben* | *to cast o's vote* |
| **'stimmen** | to tune (up); to vote |
| *das Instrument stimmen* | *to tune the instrument* |
| *stimmen (für / gegen)* | *to vote (for/against)* |
| *das stimmt* | *that's right, that's correct* |
| *das mag stimmen* | *that may be so* |
| *da stimmt etwas nicht* | *there is something wrong here* |
| *er ist gut / schlecht gestimmt* | *he is in a good/bad mood* |
| die **'Stimmung** /en | humour |
| *guter / schlechter Stimmung sein* | *to be in a good/bad mood* |
| der **Stock** s/ö-e | stick |
| *der Stock / das Stockwerk* | *floor, storey* |
| *im zweiten Stock wohnen* | *to live on the second floor* |
| *das Haus ist drei Stock hoch* | *the house is three storeys high* |
| *ein zweistöckiges Haus* | *a two-storey building* |
| der **Stoff** s/e | material; cloth; subject (matter) |
| *Stoff zu . . .* | *matter for . . .* |
| **stolz (auf)** | proud (of) |
| **'stören** | to trouble; to disturb |
| *Bitte nicht stören!* | *Please don't disturb* |
| *lassen Sie sich nicht stören!* | *don't let me disturb you!* |
| *störe ich?* | *am I disturbing you?* |
| *stör mich nicht!* | *don't bother me!* |
| **'stoßen** ie-o/ö | to push, to knock |
| die **'Strafe** /n → Belohnung | punishment; fine |

| | |
|---|---|
| *eine Strafe zahlen* | *to pay a fine* |
| *strafen* | *to punish* |
| **der Strahl** s/en | ray; beam |
| **die 'Straße** /n | street; road |
| *auf der Straße* | *in the street* |
| *über die Straße gehen* | *to cross the street* |
| *er wohnt Goethestraße 30* | *he lives at No. 30 Goethe Street* |
| *die Straßenbahn* | *tram* |
| *am Straßenrand* | *by the roadside* |
| *an der Straßenecke* | *at the street corner* |
| **'streben (nach)** | to strive (after) |
| **die 'Strecke** /n | distance |
| *eine Strecke zurücklegen* | *to cover a distance* |
| **'streichen i-i (über)** | to stroke; to pass (over); to paint |
| *von der Liste streichen* | *to strike off the roll* |
| *Frisch gestrichen!* | *Wet paint* |
| **das 'Streichholz** es/ö-er | match |
| *ein Streichholz anzünden* | *to strike a match* |
| *die Streichholzschachtel* | *matchbox* |
| **der Streit** s/Streitigkeiten | quarrel |
| *Streit anfangen (mit)* | *to start a quarrel (with)* |
| *den Streit beilegen* | *to settle the quarrel* |
| *streiten* | *to quarrel, to dispute (with)* |
| *darüber läßt sich streiten* | *that's open to question* |
| **streng** | severe, strict |
| *streng sein (gegen)* | *to be strict (with)* |
| *Streng verboten!* | *Strictly forbidden* |
| **das Stroh** s | straw |
| **der Strom** s/ö-e | (large) river; current |
| *gegen den Strom* | *against the current* |
| *mit dem Strom schwimmen* | *to go with the tide* |
| *es regnet in Strömen* | *it is pouring with rain* |
| *den Strom abschalten* | *to cut off the electricity supply* |

| | |
|---|---|
| *den Strom einschalten* | *to turn on the electricity supply* |
| **der Strumpf** s/ü-e | stocking |
| *die Strümpfe anziehen* | *to put on o's stockings* |
| *die Strümpfe ausziehen* | *to take off o's stockings* |
| **das Stück** s/e | piece; play |
| *ein Stück Brot* | *a piece of bread* |
| *ein Stück Papier* | *a piece of paper* |
| *ein Stück Seife* | *a cake of soap* |
| *Stück für Stück* | *piece by piece* |
| *ein starkes Stück!* | *that's a bit thick!* |
| *in Stücke gehen* | *to fall to pieces* |
| *in Stücke hauen* | *to knock to pieces* |
| *was für ein Stück wird gegeben?* | *what play is on?* |
| **der Stu'dent** en/en | student |
| **stu'dieren** | to study; to go to university |
| *Geschichte studieren* | *to study history* |
| *er studiert in Berlin* | *he is at university in Berlin* |
| das **'Studium** s/ien | study, studies |
| *Studien treiben* | *to study* |
| **die 'Stufe** /n | step; degree |
| *Vorsicht, Stufe!* | *Mind the step* |
| *auf gleicher Stufe mit* | *on a level with* |
| **der Stuhl** s/ü-e | chair |
| **die 'Stunde** /n | hour; lesson |
| *eine halbe Stunde* | *half an hour* |
| *anderthalb Stunden* | *one hour and a half* |
| *stundenlang* | *for hours* (*on end*) |
| *nach einer Stunde* | *after an hour* |
| *zu jeder Stunde* | *any time* |
| **der Sturm** s/ü-e | storm |
| **'stürzen** → steigen | to fall |
| *Nicht stürzen!* | *Do not drop* |
| *sich in Unkosten stürzen* | *to go to great expense* |
| **'suchen** | to seek, to look for |

| | |
|---|---|
| *Verkäuferin gesucht* | *shop assistant wanted* |
| **der 'Süden** s | south |
| *im Süden (von)* | *in/to the south (of)* |
| *in Süd . . .* | *in South . . .* |
| *nach Süden* | *south(ward)* |
| *südlich* | *south of; southern* |
| **die 'Summe** /n | sum |
| *eine hohe Summe* | *a large sum* |
| **die 'Suppe** /n | soup |
| **süß** → sauer | sweet |
| *es schmeckt süß* | *it tastes sweet, it has a sweet taste* |
| *Süßigkeiten* pl | *sweets* |
| **das Sy'stem** s/e | system |
| **die 'Szene** /n | scene |

## T

| | |
|---|---|
| **der 'Tabak** s/e | tobacco |
| **die Ta'blette** /n | tablet |
| **die 'Tafel** /n | table; (black)board |
| *eine Tafel Schokolade* | *a bar of chocolate* |
| *an die Tafel schreiben* | *to write on the blackboard* |
| **der Tag** s/e | day |
| *eines Tages* | *one day, some day* |
| *am Tage* | *by day* |
| *den ganzen Tag (lang)* | *all day (long)* |
| *jeden Tag / alle Tage* | *every day* |
| *Tag für Tag* | *day after day* |
| *von Tag zu Tag* | *from day to day* |
| *tags zuvor* | *the day before* |
| *am folgenden Tag* | *the next day* |
| *vor acht Tagen* | *a week ago* |
| *(heute) in acht Tagen* | *today week* |
| *alle acht Tage* | *every week* |
| *in vierzehn Tagen* | *in a fortnight* |
| *guten Tag!* | *how do you do? good morning/afternoon* |

| | |
|---|---|
| *welchen Tag haben wir heute?* | *what's today? what day is it (today)?* |
| **'täglich** | daily |
| **das Tal** s/ä-er → Berg | valley |
| **'tanken** | to fill up |
| *die Tankstelle* | *garage, filling station* |
| **die 'Tante** /n | aunt |
| **der Tanz** es/ä-e | dance |
| *tanzen* | *to dance* |
| **die 'Tasche** /n | pocket; bag |
| *in die Tasche stecken* | *to put in o's pocket* |
| *aus der Tasche holen* | *to take out of o's pocket* |
| **das 'Taschentuch** s/ü-er | handkerchief |
| **die 'Tasse** /n | cup |
| *eine Tasse Kaffee* | *a cup of coffee* |
| *eine Kaffeetasse* | *a coffee cup* |
| *aus der Tasse trinken* | *to drink out of a cup* |
| **tat** (1st, 3rd pers sg pret of **tun**) | |
| **die Tat** /en | action, act; deed |
| *in der Tat* | *in fact, indeed* |
| *in die Tat umsetzen* | *to put into practice* |
| **'tätig** | active |
| *die Tätigkeit* | *activity* |
| **die 'Tatsache** /n | fact |
| **tat'sächlich** | really, as a matter of fact |
| **'tausend** | a/one thousand |
| *zweitausend* | *two thousand* |
| *Tausende von Menschen* | *thousands of people* |
| **das 'Taxi** s/s | taxi |
| *Taxi frei / besetzt* | *taxi for hire/hired* |
| **'technisch** | technical |
| **der Tee** s/Teesorten | tea |
| *Tee trinken* | *to have tea* |
| **der Teil** s/e | part; share |
| *zum Teil* | *in part, partly* |
| *zum größten Teil / größtenteils* | *for the most part* |

| | |
|---|---|
| *ich für mein Teil* | *for my part, as for me* |
| *das Ersatzteil* | *spare part* |
| **'teilen** → vereinen | to divide; to share |
| *durch 5 teilen* | *to divide by 5* |
| *den Gewinn teilen* | *to share (in) the profit* |
| **'teil\|nehmen** a-o/i **(an)** | to take part (in) |
| *an einem Kurs teilnehmen* | *to take a course* |
| **teils** | in part, partly |
| **das Tele'fon** s/e (cf. **Fernsprecher)** | telephone |
| *am Telefon* | *on the phone* |
| *der (Telefon)anruf* | *(telephone) call* |
| *das Telefonbuch* | *(tele)phone directory* |
| **telefo'nieren** | to (tele)phone, to ring up, to call up |
| **das Tele'gramm** s/e | telegram |
| **der 'Teller** s/- | plate |
| *vom Teller essen* | *to eat off a plate* |
| **die Tempera'tur** / en | temperature |
| *Temperatur haben* | *to have a temperature* |
| **der 'Teppich** s/e | carpet |
| **'teuer** / teurer / am teuersten → billig | dear, expensive |
| *wie teuer ist das?* | *how much is that?* |
| *das ist (zu) teuer* | *that's (too) expensive* |
| *teuer bezahlen* | *to pay a lot (for)* |
| **das The'ater** s/- | theatre |
| *ins Theater gehen* | *to go to the theatre* |
| *die Theaterkarte* | *theatre ticket* |
| **tief** → hoch / flach | deep; low |
| *. . . ist 5 Meter tief* | *. . . is 5 metres deep* |
| *tief schlafen* | *to sleep soundly* |
| *die Tiefe* | *depth* |
| **das Tier** s/e | animal; beast |
| *wilde Tiere* | *wild beasts* |
| *ein hohes Tier* | *a "big noise", V.I.P.* |
| **der Tisch** s/e | table |
| *bei Tisch* | *at table* |

| | |
|---|---|
| *vor Tisch* | *before the meal* |
| *nach Tisch* | *after the meal* |
| *bei Tisch sitzen* | *to be at (the) table* |
| *zu Tisch, bitte!* | *dinner is served!* |
| *sich zu Tisch setzen* | *to sit down at (the) table* |
| *den Tisch decken* | *to lay the table* |
| *reinen Tisch machen* | *to make a clean sweep (of it)* |
| **die 'Tochter** /ö | daughter |
| **der Tod** es/Todesfälle → Geburt, Leben | death |
| *sich zu Tode langweilen* | *to be bored to death* |
| **die Toi'lette** /n | lavatory, W.C. |
| **toll** | mad |
| *eine tolle Sache* | *it's marvellous/wonderful* |
| **der Ton** s/ö-e | sound; tone |
| *der gute Ton* | *good form, etiquette* |
| *den Ton angeben* | *to set the tone* |
| *das Tonband* | *(recording) tape* |
| *auf Tonband aufnehmen* | *to record on tape* |
| *das Tonbandgerät* | *tape recorder* |
| **der Topf** s/ö-e | pot |
| **das Tor** s/e | door, gate; goal |
| *ein Tor schießen* | *to score a goal* |
| **tot** → lebendig | dead |
| *auf dem toten Punkt ankommen* | *to reach a deadlock* |
| **der 'Tote** n/n → Lebende | dead man |
| *die Toten* pl | *the dead* |
| *töten* | *to kill* |
| **'tragen** u-a/ä | to carry; to wear; to bear |
| *eine Brille tragen* | *to wear glasses* |
| *Früchte tragen* | *to bear fruit* |
| **der 'Traktor** s/en | tractor |
| **die 'Träne** /n | tear |
| *mit Tränen in den Augen* | *with tears in o's eyes* |
| *in Tränen ausbrechen* | *to burst into tears* |

| | |
|---|---|
| **der Traum** s/äu-e | dream |
| *einen Traum haben* | *to have a dream* |
| *träumen* | *to dream* |
| **'traurig** → froh / freudig | sad |
| **'treffen** a-o/i | to hit; to meet |
| *es traf sich, daß* | *it so happened that* |
| *ich habe ihn zu Hause getroffen* | *I found him at home* |
| *sich treffen* | *to meet* |
| *eine Verabredung treffen (mit)* | *to make an appointment* (*with*) |
| *das trifft sich gut!* | *that's lucky!* |
| **'treiben** ie-ie | to practise |
| *Sport treiben* | *to go in for sport* |
| *Handel treiben* | *to do business* |
| *was treibst du?* | *what are you doing?* |
| **'trennen** → vereinen | to separate |
| *sich trennen (von)* | *to separate* (*from*) |
| **die 'Treppe** / n | staircase |
| *auf der Treppe* | *on the staircase* |
| *ich gehe die Treppe hinauf / hinunter* | *I am going up the stairs / down the stairs* |
| **'treten** a-e/i **(auf)** | to step, to tread (on) |
| *er tritt ins Zimmer* | *he enters the room* |
| *er tritt aus dem Zimmer* | *he leaves the room* |
| *er tritt ans Fenster* | *he goes to the window* |
| *treten Sie näher!* | *step nearer* |
| *an die Stelle treten (von)* | *to take the place* (*of*) |
| **treu** | faithful, true |
| *treu bleiben* | *to remain faithful/true* (*to*) |
| **'trinken** | to drink |
| *aus einem Glas trinken* | *to drink out of a glass* |
| *ich trinke gern Wein* | *I like wine* |
| *ich trinke lieber Wein als Bier* | *I would rather have wine than beer; I prefer wine to beer* |
| *was trinken Sie?* | *what will you have* (*to drink*)? |

| | |
|---|---|
| **der Tritt** s/e | step |
| *der Fußtritt* | *kick* |
| **'trocken** → naß / feucht | dry |
| *trocken aufbewahren* | *keep dry* |
| *trocknen* | *to dry* |
| **der 'Tropfen** s/- | drop |
| *tropfenweise* | *drop by drop* |
| **der Trost** es | comfort |
| *das ist kein Trost (für mich)* | *that's no comfort (to me)* |
| *trösten* | *to comfort* |
| **trotz 'alledem** | for/in spite of all that |
| **'trotzdem** | all the same, nevertheless |
| *ich tu's trotzdem* | *I'll do it all the same* |
| **das Tuch** s/e, ü-er | cloth; scarf |
| **tun** a-a | to do; to put |
| *er tut nichts* | *he does not do anything* |
| *das tut nichts* | *it doesn't matter* |
| *was soll ich tun?* | *what am I to do?* |
| *zu tun haben (mit)* | *to have to do (with)* |
| *das tut gut* | *that does you good* |
| *er tut nur so* | *he is just pretending* |
| **die Tür** /en | door |
| *bitte Tür schließen!* | *shut the door, please* |
| *bei verschlossenen Türen* | *with the doors locked* |
| *an die Tür klopfen* | *to knock at the door* |
| *die Tür ist zu* | *the door is closed* |
| *die Tür ist angelehnt* | *the door is (left) ajar* |
| *die Tür ist offen* | *the door is open* |
| **'turnen** | to do gymnastics |

## U

| | |
|---|---|
| **'übel** → wohl | evil, bad |
| *mir ist übel* | *I feel sick* |
| *mir wird übel* | *I am going to be sick* |

| | |
|---|---|
| *das ist nicht übel* | *that's not bad* |
| *wohl oder übel* | *willy-nilly* |
| **'üben** | to exercise |
| *sich üben* | *to practise* |
| *elnen Beruf ausüben* | *to practise a profession* |
| **'überall** → nirgends | everywhere |
| *von überall her* | *from all sides* |
| **über'haupt** | generally (speaking), on the whole; at all; besides |
| *überhaupt nicht* | *not at all* |
| *überhaupt nichts* | *nothing at all* |
| **über'holen** | to pass, overtake |
| *Nicht überholen!* | *No overtaking* |
| **'übermorgen** | the day after tomorrow |
| **über'queren** | to cross |
| *die Straße überqueren* | *to cross the road* |
| **über'raschen** | to surprise |
| *die Überraschung* | *surprise* |
| *zu meiner Überraschung* | *to my surprise* |
| **über'setzen** | to translate |
| *ins Deutsche übersetzen* | *to translate into German* |
| *die Übersetzung* | *translation* |
| **über'zeugen** | to convince |
| **'übrig** | left (over), remaining, rest of |
| *das übrige Geld* | *the rest of the money* |
| *die übrigen Menschen* | *the rest of the people, the others* |
| *ich habe Geld übrig* | *I have some money left* |
| *übrig sein / übrigbleiben* | *to be left* |
| *es ist nichts übriggeblieben* | *there is nothing left* |
| *übriglassen* | *to leave (over)* |
| *laß mir was übrig* | *leave me something* |
| **'übrigens** | besides, by the way |
| die **'Übung** /en | exercise, practice |
| das **'Ufer** s/- | bank, shore |

| | |
|---|---|
| *am Ufer* | *ashore, on shore* |
| *am rechten Ufer* | *on the right bank* |
| **die Uhr** /en | watch; clock |
| *die Uhr aufziehen* | *to wind up the watch/ clock* |
| *auf die Uhr sehen* | *to look at o's watch/clock* |
| *meine Uhr geht nicht* | *my watch has stopped* |
| *meine Uhr geht richtig* | *my watch keeps good time* |
| *meine Uhr geht vor / nach* | *my watch is fast/slow* |
| *wieviel Uhr ist es?* | *what time is it?* |
| *es ist 3 Uhr* | *it is 3 o'clock* |
| *gegen 6 (Uhr)* | *about 6 (o'clock)* |
| *Punkt 6 (Uhr)* | *6 o'clock sharp* |
| *es ist halb 6 (Uhr)* | *it is half past 5* |
| *um 6 (Uhr)* | *at 6 (o'clock)* |
| *um wieviel Uhr?* | *at what time?* |
| **'um\|bringen** a-a | to kill |
| **der 'Umfang** s/ä-e | extent |
| **um'geben** a-e/i **(mit)** | to surround (with) |
| *die Umgebung* | *surroundings* |
| **um'her** | about, around |
| **'umkehren** | to return, to turn back |
| *umgekehrt* | *reverse; opposite; vice versa* |
| *umgekehrt!* | *just the other way (round)!* |
| (die) 'Umleitung /en | diversion |
| **um'sonst** | in vain; for nothing, free |
| *alles war umsonst* | *everything was useless* |
| **der 'Umstand** s/ä-e | circumstance |
| *unter diesen Umständen* | *under these circumstances* |
| *unter Umständen* | *possibly* |
| *unter keinen Umständen* | *on no account* |
| *machen Sie keine Umstände!* | *don't make a fuss!* |
| **'um\|steigen** ie-ie | to change (train, bus) |
| **'unbedingt** | definitely, absolutely |

| | |
|---|---|
| **und so 'weiter** (usw.) | and so on (etc.) |
| **der 'Unfall** s/ä-e | accident |
| *ein schwerer Unfall* | *a serious accident* |
| *bei einem Unfall* | *in an accident* |
| **'ungefähr** → genau | about, roughly |
| *ungefähr hundert* | *a hundred or so* |
| *ungefähr eine Woche* | *a week or so* |
| **'ungesund** → gesund | unhealthy |
| **das 'Unglück** s/Unglücksfälle → Glück | misfortune, accident |
| *Unglück haben* | *to be unlucky* |
| *es ist ein Unglück geschehen* | *there's been an accident* |
| *unglücklich* | *unhappy; unfortunate* |
| **'unmittelbar** / direkt | directly; immediate |
| **un'möglich** | impossible |
| **der 'Unsinn** s | nonsense |
| *Unsinn!* | *nonsense! rubbish!* |
| *mach keinen Unsinn!* | *stop fooling (about)!* |
| **'unten** → oben | below, beneath |
| *da unten* | *down there* |
| *hier unten* | *down here* |
| *unten auf der Seite* | *at the bottom of the page* |
| **'unter 'anderem** (u.a.) | among other things |
| *unter uns* | *between you and me* |
| *unter Null* | *below zero* |
| **unter'brechen** a-o/i → fortfahren, fortsetzen | to interrupt |
| **'unter\|gehen** i-a → aufgehen | to go down; to set; to sink |
| *die untergehende Sonne* | *the setting sun* |
| *die Sonne ist untergegangen* | *the sun has set* |
| **unter'halten** ie-a/ä | to entertain |
| *die Familie unterhalten* | *to maintain the family* |
| *sich unterhalten* | *to talk (to each other)* |
| *sich gut unterhalten* | *to enjoy o.s., to have a good time* |

| | |
|---|---|
| *haben Sie sich gut unterhalten?* | *did you have a nice time?* |
| **die Unter'haltung** /en | conversation |
| **unter'nehmen** a-o/i | to undertake |
| *das Unternehmen* | *firm, enterprise* |
| **der 'Unterricht** s | instruction; teaching; classes |
| *Unterricht haben* | *to have lessons* |
| **unter'scheiden** ie-ie | to distinguish |
| *sich unterscheiden (von)* | *to differ (from)* |
| **der 'Unterschied** s/e | difference |
| *ein großer Unterschied* | *a big difference* |
| *ohne Unterschied* | *alike* |
| *einen Unterschied machen* | *to make a distinction* |
| **unter'schreiben** ie-ie | to sign |
| *mit seinem Namen unterschreiben* | *to sign o's name* |
| *die Unterschrift* | *signature* |
| **unter'suchen** | to examine |
| *einen Kranken untersuchen* | *to examine a patient* |
| **die Unter'suchung** /en | test |
| *eine ärztliche Untersuchung* | *a medical examination* |
| **'unvergleichlich** | incomparable, beyond comparison |
| **'unzufrieden (mit)** → zufrieden | discontented (with) |
| **der 'Urlaub** s/e | holiday/vacation/leave |
| *auf / im Urlaub* | *on holiday/leave* |
| *Urlaub haben* | *to be on holiday/leave* |
| **die 'Ursache** /n → Wirkung | cause; reason |
| *keine Ursache!* | *don't mention it* |
| **der 'Ursprung** s/ü-e | origin |
| **das 'Urteil** s/e | judgment |
| *urteilen* | *to judge* |
| *urteilen Sie selbst!* | *judge for yourself* |
| **die USA,** *die* Vereinigten Staaten (von Amerika) *pl* | the U.S.(A.)/the United States (of America) |

# V

| | |
|---|---|
| **der 'Vater** s/ä | father |
| **(sich) ver'ändern** | to change |
| *er hat sich sehr verändert* | *he has changed a good deal* |
| *die Veränderung* | *change* |
| **ver'bergen** a-o/i → zeigen | to conceal, to hide |
| *im verborgenen* | *in secret* |
| **ver'bessern** | to improve; to correct |
| **ver'bieten** o-o → erlauben | to forbid |
| *verboten* | *forbidden, prohibited* |
| *es ist verboten (zu)* | *. . . (is) prohibited* |
| *Betreten verboten!* | *Keep off. No trespassing* |
| *Eintritt verboten!* | *No entry* |
| *Rauchen verboten!* | *No smoking* |
| **ver'binden** a-u → trennen | to connect, to combine |
| *verbinden Sie mich mit . . .* | *put me on to . . .* |
| *falsch verbunden* | *wrong number* |
| *eine Wunde verbinden* | *to dress a wound* |
| *ich bin Ihnen sehr verbunden* | *I am greatly obliged to you* |
| **die Ver'bindung** /en | union; connection |
| *sich in Verbindung setzen (mit)* | *to get in touch (with)* |
| *in Verbindung bleiben (mit)* | *to keep in touch (with)* |
| *in Verbindung stehen (mit)* | *to be in touch (with)* |
| **das Ver'brechen** s/- | crime |
| *der Verbrecher* | *criminal* |
| **ver'breiten** | to spread |
| **ver'brennen** a-a | to burn |
| *Papier verbrennen* | *to burn (up) paper* |
| *sich die Finger verbrennen* | *to burn o's fingers* |
| **ver'bringen** a-a | to spend, to pass |
| *das Wochenende verbringen* | *to spend the weekend* |

| | |
|---|---|
| *die Zeit verbringen* | *to pass the time* |
| **ver'derben** a-o/i | to spoil, to ruin |
| *jdm die Freude verderben* | *to spoil s.o's pleasure/ fun* |
| *sich den Magen verderben* | *to upset o's stomach* |
| **ver'dienen** | to earn; to deserve |
| *sein Brot verdienen* | *to earn o's living* |
| *das hat er nicht verdient* | *he didn't deserve that* |
| **ver'einen / ver'einigen** → trennen / teilen | to unite; to unify |
| *die Vereinigten Staaten* | *the United States* |
| **das Ver'fahren** s/- | process |
| **ver'folgen** | to pursue |
| *seinen Weg verfolgen* | *to go o's way* |
| **ver'gangen** (past part of **vergehen**) | past |
| **die Ver'gangenheit** | past |
| **ver'gebens** | in vain |
| *vergebens suchen* | *to search/seek in vain* |
| **ver'gehen** i-a | to pass by |
| *schnell vergehen* | *to go by quickly* |
| *vergangenes Jahr* | *last year* |
| *die Lust dazu ist mir vergangen* | *I have lost all desire for it* |
| **ver'gessen** a-e/i → sich erinnern | to forget |
| **ver'gleichen** i-i | to compare |
| *verglichen mit* | *compared to* |
| **das Ver'gnügen** s/- | pleasure |
| *mit Vergnügen* | *gladly* |
| *viel Vergnügen!* | *have a good time!* |
| *Vergnügen finden an* | *to find pleasure (in)* |
| *vergnügt* | *gay, joyous* |
| **ver'haften** | to arrest |
| **das Ver'hältnis** ses/se | relation; proportion |
| *im Verhältnis zu* | *in proportion to* |
| **die Ver'handlung** /en | negotiation |
| *in Verhandlungen treten* | *to enter into negotiations* |

| | |
|---|---|
| **ver'heiratet** → ledig | married |
| **der Ver'kauf** s/äu-e → Kauf | sale |
| *zum Verkauf anbieten* | *to offer for sale* |
| **ver'kaufen** → (ein)kaufen | to sell |
| *zu verkaufen* | *for sale, to be sold* |
| *teuer verkaufen* | *to sell at a profit* |
| *ausverkauft* | *sold out* |
| *der Verkäufer* | *seller; shop assistant* |
| **der Ver'kehr** s | traffic |
| *das Verkehrsbüro* | *tourist agency* |
| *der Verkehrsunfall* | *road accident* |
| **ver'langen** | to demand |
| *Sie werden am Telefon verlangt* | *you are wanted on the (tele)phone* |
| *auf Verlangen* | *on demand* |
| *ich habe kein Verlangen (zu)* | *I feel no desire (to)* |
| **ver'lassen** ie-a/ä → bleiben / betreten | to leave |
| *sich verlassen (auf)* | *to depend (on), to trust (in)* |
| *verlassen Sie sich darauf!* | *take it from me!* |
| *ich verlasse mich auf dich* | *I rely on you* |
| **ver'letzen** | to hurt, to injure |
| *sich verletzen* | *to hurt/injure o.s.* |
| *verletzt sein* | *to be hurt* |
| *seine Pflicht verletzen* | *to fail in o's duty* |
| **ver'lieren** o-o → finden / gewinnen | to lose |
| *seine Zeit verlieren* | *to waste o's time* |
| *der Verlust* | *loss* |
| *ein schwerer Verlust* | *a heavy loss* |
| *einen Verlust erleiden* | *to suffer a loss* |
| **ver'meiden** ie-ie | to avoid |
| *es läßt sich nicht vermeiden* | *it cannot be helped* |
| **das Ver'mögen** s/- | fortune |

| | |
|---|---|
| *ein Vermögen verdienen* | *to make a fortune* |
| **ver'muten** | to suppose, to guess |
| *vermutlich* | *presumably* |
| *er kommt vermutlich* | *I suppose he'll come* |
| **ver'nichten** → erzeugen / erhalten | to destroy |
| **ver'nünftig** | reasonable |
| *vernünftig reden* | *to talk sense* |
| **ver'passen** → erreichen | to miss |
| *ich habe den Zug verpaßt* | *I've missed the train* |
| **ver'pflichten (zu)** | to oblige (to); to engage |
| *sich verpflichten (zu)* | *to undertake* (*to*) |
| *zu Dank verpflichtet* | *obliged* |
| **ver'rückt** | mad, crazy |
| *wie verrückt* | *like mad* |
| *eine verrückte Idee* | *a crazy idea* |
| **ver'sammeln** | to gather, to assemble |
| *sich versammeln* | *to meet* |
| *die Versammlung* | *meeting* |
| *eine Versammlung abhalten* | *to hold a meeting* |
| *eine Versammlung besuchen* | *to attend a meeting* |
| **ver'schieden** → gleich | different; diverse |
| *das ist verschieden* | *that depends* |
| *verschieden sein* | *to differ* |
| *verschiedenemal* | *repeatedly* |
| **ver'schließen** o-o → öffnen | to close; to lock |
| **ver'schwinden** a-u → erscheinen | to disappear |
| **das Ver'sehen** s/- | error, mistake |
| *aus Versehen* | *by mistake* |
| **ver'sichern** | to assure |
| *die Versicherung* | *assurance; insurance* |
| **ver'sprechen** a-o/i | to promise |
| *das Versprechen* | *promise* |

| | |
|---|---|
| *sein Versprechen halten* | *to keep o's promise* |
| **der Ver'stand** s | understanding |
| *den Verstand verlieren* | *to go out of o's mind* |
| *der gesunde Menschenverstand* | *common sense* |
| **ver'standen** (past part of **verstehen**) | understood |
| **ver'stecken** → zeigen | to hide |
| *sich verstecken* | *to hide* (*o.s.*) |
| **ver'stehen** a-a | to hear; to understand; to see |
| *ich habe (es) nicht verstanden* | *I didn't hear* (*you*), *I didn't understand you* |
| *ich habe das Wort nicht verstanden* | *I didn't catch the word* |
| *ich verstehe!* | *I see!* |
| *das versteht sich* | *that goes without saying* |
| *was verstehen Sie unter . . . ?* | *what do you mean by . . .?* |
| *verstehen Sie Deutsch?* | *do you understand German?* |
| *falsch verstehen* | *to misunderstand* |
| **der Ver'such** s/e | attempt; experiment |
| **ver'suchen** | to attempt, to try |
| *den Wein versuchen* | *to taste the wine* |
| **ver'teidigen** → angreifen | to defend |
| *die Verteidigung* | *defence* |
| **das Ver'trauen** s | confidence, trust |
| *Vertrauen haben (zu)* | *to have confidence* (*in*), *to trust* |
| **ver'ursachen** | to cause; to raise |
| **ver'vollständigen** | to complete |
| **(sich) ver'wandeln** | to change/transform |
| **ver'wandt (mit)** | related (to) |
| *wir sind verwandt* | *we are related* |
| *der Verwandte* | *relative* |
| **ver'wechseln (mit)** | to confuse (with) |
| **ver'weigern** | to refuse |

| | |
|---|---|
| **ver'wenden** | to apply, to use |
| *viel Mühe verwenden (auf)* | *to go to much trouble* (*to*) |
| *viel Zeit verwenden (auf)* | *to devote much time* (*to*) |
| *etwas gut verwenden* | *to make good use of sth.* |
| **ver'wirklichen** | to realize |
| *seine Pläne verwirklichen* | *to realize o's plans* |
| **ver'wirren** → ordnen | to confuse |
| *verwirrt* | *confused* |
| **ver'wunden** | to wound |
| **das Ver'zeichnis** ses/se | list |
| **ver'zeihen** ie-ie | to forgive |
| *verzeihen Sie! / Verzeihung!* | *I beg your pardon! excuse me! sorry!* |
| *um Verzeihung bitten* | *to ask* (*s.o.'s*) *pardon* |
| **ver'zollen** | to pay duty (on) |
| *haben Sie etwas zu verzollen?* | *have you anything to declare?* |
| **das Vieh** s | cattle; beast |
| **viel** / mehr / am meisten → wenig | much |
| *nicht viel* | *not much* |
| *sehr viel* | *a great deal* (*of*) |
| *ziemlich viel* | *a good deal* (*of*) |
| *zuviel* | *too much* |
| *wieviel?* | *how much?* |
| *vielen Dank!* | *many thanks!* |
| *viel Glück!* | *good luck!* |
| *viel Vergnügen!* | *have a good time!* |
| **'viele** → wenige | many |
| *sehr viele* | *a great many* |
| *wie viele Male?* | *how often?* |
| *so viele Bücher* | *as/so many books* |
| **viel'leicht** → bestimmt | perhaps |
| **'vielmals** | many times, often |
| *danke vielmals!* | *many thanks!* |
| **'vielmehr** | rather; on the contrary |
| **das 'Viertel** s/- | quarter |

| | |
|---|---|
| *es ist viertel zwei / ein Viertel nach eins* | *it is a quarter past one* |
| *es ist dreiviertel zwei / ein Viertel vor zwei* | *it is a quarter to two* |
| *ein Viertel (¼)* | *a quarter* (*of*) |
| *dreiviertel (¾)* | *three-quarters* (*of*) |
| *ein(und)einviertel (1¼)* | *one and a quarter* |
| *ein Vierteljahr* | *three months, a quarter* (*of a year*) |
| *eine Viertelstunde* | *a quarter of an hour* |
| **der 'Vogel** s/ö | bird |
| **das Volk** s/ö-er | people, nation |
| *volkstümlich* | *popular* |
| **voll** → leer | full (of) |
| *voll Wasser* | *filled with water* |
| *voll(er) Ideen* | *full of ideas* |
| *die volle Summe* | *the entire sum* |
| *voll besetzt* | *full up, occupied* |
| **voll'enden** | to complete; to accomplish |
| *vollends* | *entirely, wholly* |
| **'völlig** | fully, completely |
| *das genügt völlig* | *that's quite enough* |
| **voll'kommen** | perfect, complete |
| *ich verstehe vollkommen* | *I understand perfectly* |
| **'vollständig** | complete, entire |
| **vor 'allem** | above all |
| **vor 'kurzem** | recently, the other day |
| *vor 8 Tagen* | *a week ago* |
| *vor einiger Zeit* | *some time ago* |
| *vor langer Zeit* | *a long time ago* |
| *es ist 10 vor eins* | *it's 10 to one* |
| **vo'raus** | ahead |
| *im voraus* | *in advance* |
| *geh voraus!* | *lead on* |
| *vorausgesetzt (daß)* | *provided* (*that*) |
| **vor'bei** | along, past; over, past |
| *er ging an mir vorbei* | *he passed me by* |

| | |
|---|---|
| *der Sommer ist vorbei* | *summer is over* |
| **'vor\|bereiten (auf)** | to prepare (for) |
| **die 'Vorderseite** /n → Rückseite | front (side) |
| **die 'Vorfahrt** | priority, right of way |
| *er hat Vorfahrt* | *he has the right of way* |
| **'vorgestern** | the day before yesterday |
| **vor'handen** | existing; present, at hand |
| *vorhanden sein* | *to exist; to be available* |
| **der 'Vorhang** s/ä-e | curtain |
| *den Vorhang auf-/zuziehen* | *to open/draw the curtain* |
| **'vorher** → hinterher, nachher | before, in advance |
| *kurz vorher* | *a short while before* |
| *am Tag vorher* | *the day before* |
| **'vorhin** | just now, a little while ago |
| **'vorig** | last |
| *voriges Jahr* | *last year* |
| **'vorläufig** | for the time being |
| **der 'Vormittag** s/e | morning, forenoon |
| *am Vormittag / vormittags* | *in the morning, a.m.* |
| *heute vormittag* | *this morning* |
| **vorn(e)** → hinten | in front, at the head |
| *nach vorn* | *forward* |
| *von vorn* | *from the front; anew* |
| **der 'Vorname** ns/n | Christian name |
| **der 'Vorrat** s/ä-e | provision, supply |
| *vorrätig* | *in store/stock* |
| **'vor\|rücken** | to advance |
| **der 'Vorschlag** s/ä-e | proposal |
| *vorschlagen* | *to propose* |
| **die 'Vorsicht** | caution, care |
| *Vorsicht!* | *Caution! Take care! Look out!* |
| *vorsichtig* | *careful* |

| | |
|---|---|
| **der 'Vorsitzende** n/n | president, chairman |
| **'vor\|stellen** | to present, to introduce; to represent |
| *ich stelle Sie ihr vor* | *I'll introduce you to her* |
| *sich (etwas) vorstellen* | *to imagine (sth.)* |
| **die 'Vorstellung** /en | performance; idea |
| *Beginn der Vorstellung um . . .* | *the performance begins at . . . , the curtain will rise at . . .* |
| **der 'Vorteil** s/e | advantage |
| *Vorteil haben (von)* | *to benefit (from)* |
| **vo'rüber** | past |
| *vorübergehen (an)* | *to pass (by)* |
| **'vorwärts** → rückwärts | forward |
| *vorwärts!* | *go ahead! let's go!* |
| **'vor\|ziehen** o-o | to prefer; to like better |
| **vor'züglich** | excellent |

## W

| | |
|---|---|
| **die 'Waage** /n | balance |
| *auf die Waage legen* | *to put on the scales* |
| **wach** | awake |
| *wach werden* | *to wake up* |
| *wachen* | *to stay awake* |
| *bei einem Kranken wachen* | *to sit up with a sick person* |
| **'wachsen** u-a/ä | to grow; to increase |
| **die 'Waffe** /n | weapon, arm(s) |
| *unter Waffen* | *under arms* |
| *zu den Waffen greifen* | *to take up arms* |
| **'wagen** | to dare, to risk |
| *sein Leben wagen* | *to risk o's neck* |
| **der 'Wagen** s/- | carriage; car |
| *mit dem Wagen fahren* | *to go by car* |
| *seinen Wagen parken* | *to park o's car* |
| *er hat seinen eigenen Wagen / selbst einen Wagen* | *he has a car of his own* |

|  |  |
|---|---|
| *der Lastwagen* | *lorry* |
| **die Wahl** /en | choice; election |
| *seine Wahl treffen* | *to take o's choice* |
| *ich habe keine Wahl* | *I have no choice* |
| **'wählen** | to choose; to elect |
| *die Nummer wählen* | *to dial the number* |
| **wahr** | true, real |
| *nicht wahr?* | *isn't it? is it not so? don't you think so?* |
| *wahr machen* | *to make sth. come true* |
| *wahr werden* | *to come true* |
| **die 'Wahrheit** /en → Lüge | truth |
| *in Wahrheit* | *in truth, in reality* |
| *die Wahrheit sagen* | *to tell the truth* |
| **wahr'scheinlich** | likely, probable, probably |
| *wahrscheinlich kommt er heute (nicht)* | *he is (un)likely to come today* |
| **der Wald** s/ä-er | forest, wood |
| **die Wand** /ä-e | wall |
| *in seinen vier Wänden* | *at home* |
| **'wandern** | to wander, to walk |
| **die 'Wange** /n | cheek |
| *rotwangig* | *rosy-cheeked* |
| **wann** | when |
| *wann kommst du?* | *when will you come?* |
| *bis wann?* | *till when? by what time?* |
| *seit wann?* | *how long? since when?* |
| *wann auch immer* | *whenever* |
| *dann und wann* | *now and then* |
| *wann sind Sie geboren?* | *when were you born?* |
| **war, 'waren** (1st, 3rd pers sg, pl pret of **sein**) | was, were |
| **die 'Ware** /n | ware, article |
| *das Warenhaus* | *store(s)* |
| **warm** / wärmer / am wärmsten → kalt | warm |

| | |
|---|---|
| *es ist warm* | *it is warm* |
| *mir ist warm* | *I am warm* |
| *es wird warm* | *it is getting warm* |
| *sich wärmen* | *to warm o.s.* |
| **die 'Wärme** → Kälte | warmth |
| **'warnen (vor)** | to warn (of, against) |
| *Vor Taschendieben wird gewarnt!* | *Beware of pickpockets* |
| **'warten (auf)** | to wait (for) |
| *warten lassen* | *to keep (s.o.) waiting* |
| *auf sich warten lassen* | *to be long in coming* |
| **wa'rum** | why |
| *warum nicht?* | *why not?* |
| **was** | what |
| *was ist das?* | *what's this?* |
| *was für ein . . .?* | *what (kind of) . . .?* |
| *was für ein . . .!* | *what (a) . . .!* |
| *was kostet das?* | *how much is that?* |
| **'waschen** u-a/ä | to wash |
| *sich waschen* | *to wash (o.s.)* |
| *der Waschlappen* | *face-cloth* |
| **die 'Wäsche** | linen, washing; underwear |
| *frische Wäsche anziehen* | *to change o's underclothes* |
| **das 'Wasser** s/- | water |
| *ein Glas Wasser* | *a glass of water* |
| *warmes Wasser* | *hot water* |
| *mit fließendem Wasser* | *with running water* |
| *mit kaltem Wasser* | *with cold water* |
| *das Wasser kocht* | *the water is boiling* |
| **die 'Watte** | cotton-wool |
| **das W.C.** | W.C., lavatory |
| **der 'Wechsel** s/- | change |
| *die Wechselstube* | *foreign exchange bureau* |
| *wechseln* | *to change* |
| *Geld wechseln* | *to exchange money* |
| *können Sie 100 Mark wechseln?* | *can you exchange/give me change for 100 marks?* |

| | |
|---|---|
| **'wecken** | to wake up |
| **'weder . . . 'noch** | neither . . . nor |
| **der Weg** s/e | way, road |
| *der Weg nach Berlin* | *the way to Berlin* |
| *der Weg zum Bahnhof* | *the way to the station* |
| *den Weg zeigen* | *to show the way* |
| *einen Weg einschlagen* | *to take a road* |
| *einen Weg fahren* | *to follow a road/route* |
| *sich auf den Weg machen* | *to set out* (*for*) |
| *der richtige Weg (nach)* | *the right way* (*to*) |
| *nach dem Weg fragen* | *to ask the way* |
| **weg** → da | away, off |
| *er ist weg* | *he is gone* |
| *das Buch ist weg* | *the book is lost* |
| *Hände weg!* | *hands off!* |
| **'weg\|fahren** u-a/ä, **'weg\|gehen** i-a → zurückkehren | to go away, to leave |
| *das geht weg* | *that'll pass off* |
| **'weg\|laufen** ie-au/äu | to run away |
| **'weg\|nehmen** a-o/i | to take away |
| **'weg\|schaffen** | to remove |
| **weh** | sore |
| *es tut mir weh* | *it hurts me* |
| *wo tut es (Ihnen) weh?* | *where does it hurt?* |
| *der Kopf tut mir weh* | *my head aches* |
| *er hat mir wehgetan* | *he has hurt me* |
| **'wehen** | to blow |
| *der Wind weht* | *the wind is blowing* |
| *die Fahne weht* | *the flag is flying* |
| **'weiblich** | feminine; female |
| **weich** → hart / fest | soft; tender |
| **'Weihnachten** | Christmas |
| *zu Weihnachten* | *at Christmas* |
| *Fröhliche Weihnachten!* | *Merry Christmas!* |
| **die 'Weile** | while |
| *eine Weile* | *for a while* |
| *eine ganze Weile* | *quite a while* |

| | |
|---|---|
| *nach einer Weile* | *after a while* |
| *bleib noch eine Weile!* | *stay a bit longer* |
| **der Wein** s/e | wine; vine; grapes |
| *ein Glas Wein* | *a glass of wine* |
| *das Weinglas* | *the wine glass* |
| *Wein trinken* | *to drink wine* |
| *den Wein kosten* | *to taste the wine* |
| **'weinen** → lachen | to weep, to cry |
| **'weise** → dumm | wise |
| *die Weisheit* | *wisdom* |
| **die 'Weise** /n | way |
| *auf welche Weise?* | *in what way?* |
| *auf diese Weise* | *in this way* |
| *in keiner Weise* | *in no way* |
| **weiß** | white |
| **weiß** (1st, 3rd pers sg pres of **wissen**) | know(s) |
| **weit** → nahe / eng | far; wide, large, broad |
| *ich bin so weit* | *I am ready* |
| *das geht zu weit* | *that's going too far* |
| *es ist weit von hier* | *it is a long way from here* |
| *weit und breit* | *far and wide* |
| *weit weg* | *a long way off* |
| *ist es noch weit?* | *is it still a long way?* |
| *wie weit ist es nach ...?* | *how far is it to ...?* |
| *von weitem* | *from a distance* |
| *bei weitem / weitaus* | *by far, much* |
| **'weiter** → näher | farther, further |
| *nichts weiter* | *that's all, nothing else* |
| *weiter niemand* | *no one else* |
| *und so weiter* | *and so on* |
| **'weiter\|gehen i-a** → stehenbleiben | to go on |
| **der 'Weizen s/** Weizensorten | wheat |
| **'welche(r,s)** | what, which (one) |
| **die Welt** /en | world |

| | |
|---|---|
| *die ganze Welt* | *the whole world* |
| *in der ganzen Welt* | *all over the world* |
| *auf die Welt kommen* | *to come into the world* |
| **wem** | to whom |
| **wen** | whom |
| **'wenden** | to turn |
| *Bitte wenden!* | *Please turn over* |
| *sich wenden (an)* | *to turn (to)* |
| *die Seite umwenden* | *to turn over the page* |
| **'wenig** → viel | little, few |
| *ein wenig* | *a little* |
| *wenig Zeit* | *little time* |
| *ein wenig Geduld* | *a little patience* |
| *zu wenig Geld* | *too little money* |
| *wenig Leute* | *few people* |
| **'weniger (als)** → mehr (als) | less (than) |
| *viel weniger* | *much less* |
| *mehr oder weniger* | *more or less* |
| *immer weniger* | *less and less* |
| *5 weniger 3 ist 2* | *5 minus 3 equals 2* |
| **'wenigstens** → höchstens | at least |
| **wer** | who |
| *wer ist da?* | *who is there?* |
| *wer ist das?* | *who is he?* |
| **'werden** u-o/i | to become; to get; to grow |
| *es wird kalt* | *it is getting cold* |
| *es wird schon werden* | *it will be all right* |
| *das muß anders werden* | *there must be a change* |
| **'werfen** a-o/i | to throw |
| **das Werk** s/e | work; works |
| *sich ans Werk machen* | *to set to work* |
| *Goethes Werke* | *Goethe's works* |
| *die Werkstatt* | *workshop* |
| *das Werkzeug* | *tool* |
| **wert** | worth |
| *wert sein* | *to be worth* |

| | |
|---|---|
| *das ist nichts wert* | *that's no good* |
| *das ist nicht viel wert* | *that's not up to much* |
| *das ist nicht der Rede wert* | *it's not worth mentioning* |
| **der Wert** s/e | value; worth |
| *Wert legen auf* | *to make much of, stress* |
| **das 'Wesen** s/- | being; nature |
| *ein lebendes Wesen* | *a living creature* |
| *sein Wesen gefällt mir* | *I like his manners* |
| **'wesentlich** | essential |
| *die wesentlichen Merkmale* | *the essential features* |
| **der 'Westen** s | west |
| *im Westen (von)* | *in/to the west (of)* |
| *westlich* | *west (of), western* |
| **das 'Wetter** s/- | weather |
| *es ist schönes Wetter* | *it's lovely weather* |
| *bei schlechtem / schönem Wetter* | *in bad/fine weather* |
| *wie ist heute das Wetter?* | *how is the weather today?* |
| *bei solchem Wetter* | *in such weather* |
| **'wichtig** → unwichtig | important |
| *es ist für mich sehr wichtig* | *it's of great importance to me* |
| *nichts Wichtiges* | *nothing that matters* |
| *die Wichtigkeit* | *importance* |
| *von größter Wichtigkeit* | *of the greatest importance* |
| **wider'stehen** a-a | to resist |
| *Widerstand leisten* | *to offer resistance* |
| **wie** | how |
| *wie geht es Ihnen?* | *how do you do? how are you?* |
| *wie lange (noch)?* | *how much longer?* |
| *wie lange (schon)?* | *how long?* |
| *wie bitte?* | *I beg your pardon?* |
| *wie schön das ist!* | *how beautiful it is!* |
| *wie groß er ist!* | *how tall he is!* |

| | |
|---|---|
| *wie interessant!* | *how interesting!* |
| *wie schade!* | *what a pity!* |
| *wie zum Beispiel* | *such as for example* |
| **'wieder** | again |
| *immer wieder* | *again and again* |
| *nie wieder* | *never again* |
| **wieder'holen** | to repeat |
| *wiederholt* | *repeatedly* |
| *die Wiederholung* | *repetition* |
| **'wieder\|sehen** a-e/ie | to see again |
| *(auf) Wiedersehen!* | *goodbye! so long!* |
| **'wiegen** o-o | to weigh |
| *das Päckchen wiegt . . .* | *the parcel weighs . . .* |
| **die 'Wiese** /n | meadow |
| **wie'so** | how, why (so), but why |
| **wie'viel** | how much, how many |
| *wieviel kosten die Äpfel?* | *how much are these apples?* |
| *wieviel ist 2 + 2?* | *how much is 2 + 2?* |
| *wieviel Personen?* | *how many people?* |
| *wieviel Blumen!* | *what a lot of flowers!* |
| *wieviel Uhr ist es?* | *what's the time?* |
| *den wievielten haben wir heute?* | *what is the date today?* |
| **wild** | wild |
| *wilde Tiere* | *wild animals* |
| **will** (1st, 3rd pers sg pres of **wollen**) | |
| **der 'Wille** ns/n | will |
| *guten Willens sein* | *to have good intentions* |
| *um . . . willen* | *for the sake of . . .* |
| **will'kommen** | welcome |
| *seien Sie willkommen!* | *welcome!* |
| *willkommen heißen* | *to welcome* |
| **willst** (2nd pers sg pres of **wollen**) | |
| **der Wind** s/e | wind |

| | |
|---|---|
| *draußen geht ein Wind* | *there is a wind blowing outside* |
| **'winken** | to wave |
| *mit der Hand winken* | *to wave o's hand* |
| *mit dem Taschentuch winken* | *to wave o's handkerchief* |
| **der 'Winter** s/- | winter |
| *im Winter* | *in winter* |
| **wir** Deutschen | we Germans |
| **wird** (3rd pers sg pres of **werden**) | |
| **'wirken (auf)** | to act (on); to operate; to take effect |
| *das Mittel wirkt* | *the remedy takes (effect)/ is effective* |
| **'wirklich** → unwirklich | real(ly) |
| *die Wirklichkeit* | *reality* |
| *in Wirklichkeit* | *in reality* |
| *wirksam* | *effective* |
| **die 'Wirkung** /en | effect; action |
| *eine Wirkung haben* | *to produce an effect* |
| **die 'Wirtschaft** /en | household; economy |
| *sie führt ihm die Wirtschaft* | *she runs his household* |
| *wirtschaftlich* | *economic(al)* |
| **'wischen** | to wipe (clean), to clean |
| *die Tafel abwischen* | *to wipe the blackboard* |
| *sich das Gesicht abwischen* | *to wipe o's face* |
| **'wissen** u-u/ei | to know |
| *ich möchte wissen* | *I wonder, I would like to know* |
| *man kann nie wissen* | *you never know* |
| *soviel ich weiß* | *for all I know* |
| *ich weiß nichts davon* | *I don't know anything about it* |
| *das Wissen* | *knowledge; learning* |
| *meines Wissens* | *as far as I know* |

| | |
|---|---|
| *nach bestem Wissen und Gewissen* | *to the best of o's knowledge and belief* |
| **die 'Wissenschaft** /en | science |
| **wo** | where |
| **die 'Woche** /n | week |
| *nächste Woche* | *next week* |
| *vor einer Woche* | *a week ago* |
| *letzte Woche* | *last week* |
| *wöchentlich* | *weekly* |
| **das 'Wochenende** s | weekend |
| **der 'Wochentag** s/e | weekday |
| **wo'her** | from where |
| **wo'hin** | where (to) |
| **wohl** → übel | well |
| *sich wohl fühlen* | *to be well* |
| *mir ist nicht wohl* | *I don't feel well* |
| *leben Sie wohl!* | *goodbye!* |
| *auf Ihr Wohl!* | *here's to you!* |
| **'wohnen** | to live |
| *in der Stadt wohnen* | *to live in the town* |
| *auf dem Lande wohnen* | *to live in the country* |
| *ich wohne in der Goethestraße* | *I live in Goethe Street* |
| *ich wohne Goethestraße 3* | *I live at No. 3 Goethe Street* |
| *er wohnt bei mir* | *he lives/is staying with me* |
| **die 'Wohnung** /en | flat; residence |
| *das Wohnzimmer* | *sitting-room* |
| **die 'Wolke** /n | cloud |
| **die 'Wolle** | wool |
| *aus Wolle* | *woollen, made of wool* |
| **'wollen** o-o/i | to want |
| *lieber wollen* | *to prefer* |
| *(ganz) wie Sie wollen* | *(just) as you like* |
| *zu wem wollen Sie?* | *whom do you want to see?* |
| **wo'mit** | with what |

| | |
|---|---|
| **wo'ran** | at/of/in what |
| *woran denkst du?* | *what are you thinking about/of?* |
| **'worden** (*past* part of werden) | |
| **das Wort** es/ö-er; e | word |
| *ein offenes Wort sprechen* | *to speak frankly* |
| *kein Wort sprechen* | *to keep silent* |
| *Wort halten* | *to keep o's word* |
| *das Wort ergreifen* | *to (begin to) speak* |
| *sein Wort brechen* | *to break o's word* |
| *beim Wort nehmen* | *to take* (*s.o.*) *at his word* |
| *mit einem Wort* | *in a word* |
| *mit anderen Worten* | *in other words* |
| **die 'Wunde** /n | wound |
| *eine Wunde verbinden* | *to dress a wound* |
| **sich 'wundern (über)** | to be surprised (at) |
| *es wundert mich* | *I am surprised* |
| **der Wunsch** s/ü-e | wish, desire |
| *haben Sie noch einen Wunsch?* | *is there anything else you'd like?* |
| *mit den besten Wünschen* | *with best wishes* |
| **'wünschen** | to wish, to desire, to want |
| *wünschen Sie noch etwas?* | *would you like anything else?* |
| *das läßt zu wünschen übrig* | *that leaves something to to be desired* |
| *Glück wünschen* | *to wish* (*s.o.*) *luck* |
| **'wurde** (1st, 3rd pers sg pret of **werden**) | |
| **'würde** (1st, 3rd pers sg cond of **werden**) | |
| **die 'Würde** | dignity |
| **'würdig** → unwürdig | worthy |
| **die Wurst** /ü-e | sausage |
| **die 'Wurzel** /n | root |
| *Wurzel schlagen* | *to take root* |

| | |
|---|---|
| **'wußte** (1st, 3rd pers sg pret of **wissen**) | knew |
| **die 'Wüste** /n | desert |
| **die Wut** | rage |
| *wütend sein* | *to be in a rage* |
| *wütend werden* | *to lose o's temper* |

## Z

| | |
|---|---|
| **die Zahl** /en | number; figure |
| *in großer Zahl* | *in large numbers* |
| *Zahlen zusammenzählen* | *to add up figures* |
| *zahlreich* | *numerous* |
| **'zahlen** | to pay |
| *zahlen, bitte!* | *the bill, please!* |
| **'zählen** | to count |
| *das zählt nicht* | *that does not count* |
| *ich zähle auf dich* | *I am counting on you* |
| *an den Fingern abzählen* | *to count on o's fingers* |
| **der Zahn** s/ä-e | tooth |
| *die Zähne putzen* | *to brush o's teeth* |
| *sich einen Zahn ziehen lassen* | *to have a tooth out* |
| *der Zahnarzt* | *dentist* |
| *zum Zahnarzt gehen* | *to go to the dentist's* |
| *die Zahnbürste* | *toothbrush* |
| *Zahnschmerzen haben* | *to have toothache* |
| *die Zahnpasta* | *toothpaste* |
| **zart** | delicate; tender |
| **die 'Zehe** /n | toe |
| *auf Zehenspitzen* | *on tiptoe* |
| **das 'Zeichen** s/- | sign; signal |
| *ein Zeichen geben* | *to make a sign* |
| *das Zeichen abwarten* | *to wait for the signal* |
| *das Verkehrszeichen* | *traffic sign* |
| **'zeichnen** | to draw |
| **'zeigen** | to show, to point |

| | |
|---|---|
| *das wird sich zeigen* | *we shall see* |
| *die Papiere zeigen* | *to show o's papers* |
| die 'Zeile /n | line |
| *schreib / schreiben Sie mir ein paar Zeilen* | *drop me a line* |
| die Zeit /en | time |
| *zur Zeit* | *at the present time* |
| *zur (rechten) Zeit kommen* | *to arrive in good time* |
| *zur gleichen Zeit* | *at the same time* |
| *die ganze Zeit* | *all the time* |
| *vor langer Zeit* | *a long time ago* |
| *nach einiger Zeit* | *some time afterwards* |
| *kurze Zeit danach* | *shortly after* |
| *um welche Zeit?* | *at what time?* |
| *von Zeit zu Zeit* | *from time to time* |
| *Zeit haben* | *to have (plenty of) time* |
| *ich habe keine Zeit* | *I have no time* |
| *es ist höchste Zeit* | *it is high time* |
| *lassen Sie sich Zeit* | *take your time (about it)* |
| *seine Zeit verbringen* | *to pass o's time* |
| *zeitig* | *early* |
| *zeitig aufstehen* | *to get up early* |
| die 'Zeitung /en | (news)paper |
| *die Zeitung lesen* | *to read the paper* |
| das Zelt s/e | tent |
| zer'brechen a-o/i | to break (in two) |
| zer'reißen i-i | to tear; to tear to pieces |
| zer'schlagen u-a/ä | to break (to pieces) |
| zer'stören | to destroy, to demolish, to ruin |
| der 'Zettel s/- | label; slip (of paper) |
| das Zeug s | thing(s) |
| *dummes Zeug reden* | *to talk nonsense* |
| 'ziehen o-o → schieben | to pull; to draw |
| *den Griff ziehen* | *to pull the handle* |

| | |
|---|---|
| *eine Linie ziehen* | *to draw a line* |
| *in Zweifel ziehen* | *to doubt* |
| *hier zieht es* | *there is a draught here* |
| **das Ziel** s/e | aim; finish |
| *das Ziel erreichen* | *to achieve o's aim* |
| *das Ziel verfehlen* | *to miss the mark* |
| *(sich) ein Ziel setzen* | *to set* (*o.s.*) *an aim* |
| **'ziemlich** | rather |
| *ziemlich gut* | *pretty good* |
| *ziemlich viel* | *quite a lot* (*of*) |
| **die Ziga'rette** /n | cigarette |
| *eine Zigarette rauchen* | *to smoke a cigarette* |
| *eine Zigarette anzünden* | *to light a cigarette* |
| **die Zi'garre** /n | cigar |
| **das 'Zimmer** s/- | room |
| *Zimmer zu vermieten* | *Room to let* |
| *das Zimmer geht auf den Garten (hinaus)* | *the room faces the garden* |
| *ist ein Zimmer frei?* | *is there a room vacant?* |
| **'zittern (vor)** | to tremble, to shake (with) |
| **der Zoll** s/ö-e | customs |
| *die Zollkontrolle* | *customs inspection* |
| **die 'Zone** /n | zone |
| **zu** → offen | closed, shut |
| *Tür zu!* | *Shut the door!* |
| **der 'Zucker** s/- | sugar |
| **'zu\|decken (mit)** → aufdecken | to cover (with) |
| **zu'erst** → zuletzt | at first, first of all; first; to begin with |
| **'zufällig** → absichtlich | by chance |
| *zufällig etwas tun* | *to happen to be doing sth.* |
| **zu'frieden** | content, satisfied |
| *zufrieden sein (mit)* | *to be satisfied* |
| **der Zug** s/ü-e | train |
| *mit dem Zug* | *by train* |

| | |
|---|---|
| *mit dem Zug fahren* | *to go by train* |
| *den Zug verpassen* | *to miss the train* |
| *der Personenzug* | *stopping train* |
| *der Schnellzug* | *express (train)* |
| **zu'gleich** → nacheinander | at the same time; together |
| **'zu\|hören** | to listen |
| *hör mal (zu)!* | *listen!* |
| **die 'Zukunft** | future |
| *in Zukunft* | *in (the) future* |
| **zu'letzt** → zuerst | in the end, at last; last |
| *er kam zuletzt* | *he came last* |
| **'zu\|machen** → öffnen | to shut, to close |
| **zu'nächst** | first of all, to begin with |
| **die 'Zunge** /n | tongue |
| **zu'rück** | back |
| *zurück!* | *go back!* |
| *er ist noch nicht zurück* | *he hasn't come back yet* |
| **zu'rück\|kehren** → weggehen | to return; to come back |
| **zu'sammen** → einzeln / getrennt | (al)together |
| **zu'sammen\|setzen** | to compose, to assemble; to put together |
| **der 'Zuschauer** s/- | spectator; (tele)viewer |
| **'zu\|schließen** o-o → aufschließen | to lock (up) |
| **der 'Zustand** s/ä-e | state; condition |
| *in gutem Zustand* | *in good condition* |
| **der 'Zutritt** s | access; admission |
| *Zutritt verboten!* | *No admittance* |
| **zu'viel(e)** | too much/many |
| *viel zuviel* | *far too much* |
| *das ist zuviel!* | *that's really too much!* |
| **zu'weilen** | sometimes |
| **zwar** | to be sure, it's true |
| *und zwar* | *namely* |

| | |
|---|---|
| **der Zweck** s/e | aim, purpose |
| *zu diesem Zweck* | *for this purpose* |
| *zu welchem Zweck?* | *what for?* |
| *das hat keinen Zweck* | *that's pointless, of no use* |
| **der 'Zweifel** s/- | doubt |
| *ohne Zweifel* | *no doubt, doubtless* |
| *darüber besteht kein Zweifel* | *there is no doubt about it* |
| *zweifellos* | *doubtless* |
| *zweifeln* | *to doubt* |
| **der Zweig** s/e | branch |
| **'zwingen** a-u | to force |

## Die Wochentage/The days of the week

| | |
|---|---|
| 'Sonntag | Sunday |
| 'Montag | Monday |
| *am Montag, montags* | *on Monday*(*s*) |
| 'Dienstag | Tuesday |
| 'Mittwoch | Wednesday |
| 'Donnerstag | Thursday |
| 'Freitag | Friday |
| 'Sonnabend, 'Samstag | Saturday |

## Die Monate/The months

| | |
|---|---|
| 'Januar | January |
| *im Januar* | *in January* |
| *Mitte Januar* | *in mid-January* |
| *Ende Januar* | *in late January* |
| 'Februar | February |
| März | March |
| A'pril | April |
| Mai | May |
| 'Juni | June |
| 'Juli | July |
| Au'gust | August |
| Sep'tember | September |
| Ok'tober | October |
| No'vember | November |
| De'zember | December |

# Bibliography

F. Wilhelm Kaeding, *Häufigkeitswörterbuch der deutschen Sprache*. Steglitz, 1897; Berlin, 1898.

W. Horn, *Basic Writing Vocabulary*. Berlin, 1926.

B. Q. Morgan, *German Frequency Word Book*. New York, 1928, 1931.

*Interim Report on Vocabulary Frequency*. London, 1930/31.

Harald E. Palmer, *Second Interim Report on Vocabulary Selection*. Tokyo, 1931.

Hugo Bakonyi, *Die gebräuchlichsten Wörter der deutschen Sprache*. Munich, 1933, 1939.

Carnegie-Konferenz 1934/35, publ. 1936: *Interim Report on Vocabulary Selection*.

C. K. Ogden, *The General Basic English Dictionary*. 1940, 1957/13.

Michael West, *A General Service List of English Words*. 1953.

M. Auber, *Le Vocabulaire pour Baccalauréats. Guide de fréquence. Allemand*. n.d.

Walter Schultze, *Der Wortschatz in der Grundschule*. Stuttgart, 1956.

*Wortschatzminimum der deutschen Sprache für die Mittelschule*. Moscow, 1957.

René Michéa, *Vocabulaire Allemand Progressif*. Paris, 1959.

*Kinderduden*. Mannheim, 1959.

Alfred Haase, *Englisches Arbeitswörterbuch*. Frankfurt (Main), 1959, 1691/2.

I. W. Rachmanow, *Wörterbuch der meistgebrauchten Wörter der englischen, deutschen und französischen Sprache*. Moscow, 1960.

R. Zellweger, *Le vocabulaire du bachelier. 3000 mots allemands choisies et présentés*. Lausanne, 1962.

Hans-Heinrich Wängler, *Rangwörterbuch hochdeutscher Umgangssprache*. Marburg, 1963.

Eliane Kaufholz, Marc Zemb, H. Neuss, *Vocabulaire de Base de l'Allemand*. Paris, 1963.
Erich Weis, *Grund- und Aufbauwortschatz Englisch*. Stuttgart, 1964.
Helmut Meier, *Deutsche Sprachstatistik*. Hildesheim, 1964.
J. Allen Pfeffer, *Grunddeutsch Basic (Spoken) German Word List, Grundstufe*. New Jersey, 1964.
*Německé Základní Lexikální Minimum*. Prague, 1965.
Michael West, *An International Reader's Dictionary*. London, 1966.